The Dueling Personas of Kevin Smith

Copyright © 2003 Matthew Miller

All rights reserved. This book may not be reproduced in whole or in part in any form or format without written permission of the publisher.

Published by:
View Askew Books
3 Harding Road
Red Bank, NJ
07701

ISBN: 0-9725264-0-4

Visit us on the web at www.viewaskew.com

Contents

Preface
4

Introduction
7

The Creation of the Author(s)
17

Chasing Amy and the Integration/Division
of Smith's Personas
41

An Author Divided
55

Blurring the Line
73

Conclusion
95

Notes
99

Bibliography
103

Websites Consulted
111

For Keli

Preface

Looking back, I wish that I could say that this book's origins lay in something noble, like pure intellectual curiosity or a quest to contribute knowledge to the discipline of film studies. And, while I'd like to think that both of those drives played a part in the research and writing of the book you're holding, the truth is that my initial motivations for writing at length about Kevin Smith were rooted in something a bit baser—sheer panic.

When I started my first class of graduate school, I had never written a paper longer than 15 pages (well, there was that 25-page group paper in which most of my co-writers decided that their time in group meetings would be better spent developing the perfect gravity bong than writing, but that's another story). So when I looked at the syllabus and saw that in less than 3 months I would be required to turn in a 35-45 page term paper on film history, I'm not exaggerating when I say that a real sense of dread began to set in. 35? What could I possibly have to say that would fill 35 pages? Even with a Courier font and some conspicuously thick margins, that was going to be tough.

In the next couple of weeks a lot of different ideas fluttered around in my head—a history of the critical reception of David Lynch's films, a look at the unusual popularity of Hong Kong kung-fu films in the African American community since the 1970s, a history of Stephen King adaptations—but none really made me excited to set pen to paper. Not until I read the following passage in Robert Allen and Douglas Gomery's *Film*

History: Theory and Practice, that is:

> Most popular culture products are produced by authors "without biographies" in the sense that to their audiences they are anonymous. Their names signify nothing beyond the credit line at the beginning of their films; they have no persona outside of their films…There are other authors, however, who are known not only as credit lines on their films, but also as public figures. The facts of their lives, their production practices, and their pronouncements are conveyed to the public via journalists, reviewers, their own publicists, advertising materials for their films, memoirs, and, most recently, television talk shows. Their resulting "biographical legends"…become an important historical background for reading their films, and, in fact, frequently become inscribed in their films as well (Allen & Gomery, 88-9).

I instantly realized that there was one director whose 'biographical legend' I'd been constantly exposed to for years—Kevin Smith.

Smith's first two films had been practically ubiquitous in the dorm rooms of my friends and I while I'd been in college in Chapel Hill, North Carolina. We quoted his character's garrulous profanities incessantly (which, in retrospect, probably explains why we didn't have girlfriends at the time…), our monologues flawless thanks to repeated late night viewings. We all liked his first film, *Clerks*, but it was *Mallrats*, his second film, that you were more likely to find us making arcane references to. And, if you had asked us why we were so engaged with that film, any one of us probably would have answered the same: *'Rats* made it obvious that Kevin Smith was one of us. He had obviously grown up reading the same comic books that we had, and could probably wax intellectual about the relative merits of various superpowers. He, too, referred to

Star Wars as 'The Trilogy' and could likely tell you the name of the fat guy in the first one who, during the raid on the Death Star, kept saying, "Stay on target!" In short, he seemed like the kind of guy that a bunch of college sophomores like us would like to hang out with and get to know.

And, as the next few years passed, I found that you practically could get to know him. He gave interviews left and right. He had a website that he posted to all of the time. And all of the impressions we had gotten about him from his films were confirmed.

Most of my friends moved past their fascination with Kevin Smith (I think a lot of them watch *Buffy* now…), but I continued to be intrigued by him. I followed his move into comics, his expanding Internet presence, and especially his increasingly self-reflexive films. All of which, I realized, was a perfect example of a director building his own biographical legend—easily 35 pages worth. And when I shared my ideas for my paper with my colleagues, the idea really took shape.

Because the Kevin Smith that they knew of was completely different from the one that I had been exposed to for years. And this book is the ultimate result of me trying to determine why. I hope you enjoy reading it as much as I enjoyed researching and writing it.

Essentially, the book you're holding is my Master's thesis, and I would be remiss without thanking Emory University and their excellent film studies program for allowing me to pursue a topic that many in academia would likely consider unworthy of study. Special thanks go out to Drs. Matthew Bernstein and Nina Martin, my thesis advisors. Without their guidance, this book wouldn't be half of what it is. My deepest gratitude also goes out to Keli Decker, my girlfriend, for if it wasn't for her, the only copy of this would be the one on my shelf. She's put up with a lot from me, and thanking her in print is the least I can do. Finally, thank you to Kevin Smith for reading this in the first place, much less making it possible for others to do the same. I am truly in awe of your generosity.

Introduction

In March of 2000, *Esquire* magazine, positing that the current crop of young filmmakers was the most talented since the rise of the 'New Hollywood' auteurs of the 1970s, asked several film critics and Martin Scorsese to name "the next Scorsese." The first article in the series was written by arguably the most prominent of the critics, Andrew Sarris, who gained recognition in the 1960s by importing the French auteur 'theory' to America. Sarris named 30-year-old writer/director Kevin Smith as the most likely to assume Scorsese's auteurist throne. Interestingly, Sarris did not base his decision primarily on the merits of Smith's filmic oeuvre. "I must confess," he wrote, "that I have been overwhelmed by only one of Smith's four films," *Chasing Amy* (Miramax, 1997). Instead, Sarris chose Smith for his "flair for merchandising" and his broad-based appeal. "What is most striking about Smith is that he is so good a writer and at the same time fully in tune with the subliterate tastes of young audiences," Sarris noted, adding, "His cultural ambidextrousness bodes well for his future" (Sarris 2000, 218). It is Smith's 'cultural ambidextrousness' that this book will explore in greater depth. Kevin Smith is a cinematic Janus, able to make films that communicate to both the critical establishment and to a fan culture, often during the same film, and, sometimes, during the same scene.

In this book, I will first detail the career of Kevin Smith in the eyes of the critical establishment in the wake of *Clerks* (Miramax, 1994), focusing on the ways in which he initially shaped his biography to appeal to critics, the failure to ground his second film, *Mallrats* (Gramercy, 1995), in that biography, and the reclaiming of that critical biography in his third film, *Chasing Amy* (Miramax, 1997). After the critical and financial failure of *Mallrats*, *Chasing Amy* was expressly designed, in part, to prompt critics to recall the parts of his *Clerks*-era biography that they initially praised.

Kevin Smith's persona took on a new facet, as I will show, in the creation of a second biography for Smith—that of 'fanboy.' This biography, rooted in comic books and a comic book culture, arose in response to Smith's ties to comics, ties that are made clear in *Mallrats*. Critics missed this persona, as, in the film, Smith uses a manner of address that talks specifically to a comic book-savvy audience. This audience, in turn, formed the core of Smith's own sizeable fan base, around which a full-fledged fandom would coalesce. Smith would continue this 'fanboy' persona with *Chasing Amy*, using many of the same strategies he employed in *Mallrats* to please fans.

Chasing Amy, then, was designed to appeal to both critics and fans by priming each of Smith's respective biographies. Detailed textual analysis indicates that Smith, through the film's subplot, uses *Chasing Amy* as both a meditation upon and a mediation of these two biographies. The narrative resolution of the film finds Smith's critical persona winning out while the 'fanboy' persona is disavowed. This was instrumental in prompting critics to reembrace Smith and to approach his subsequent film, *Dogma* (Lions Gate, 1999), with his critical biography in mind.

Smith's 'fanboy' biography, however, did not disappear after being defeated in *Chasing Amy*. Rather, Smith returned the 'fanboy' to its roots, beginning a secondary career writing comic books. As comics are a medium largely ignored by most critics, Smith was free to express all of the tendencies that critics disliked about *Mallrats*. The increasingly fan-savvy Smith also employed the Internet, DVD technology and merchandising in a successful effort to foster the coalescence of a fan base. By Smith's fifth film, *Jay and Silent Bob Strike Back*

(Dimension, 2001), the boundaries dividing the personas had begun to blur, but Smith remained conscious of each persona and the ways in which they function. As a result, he was still largely able to please both critics and fans, in spite of the fact that the film contains elements that could have sparked dissent from either camp.

Through these arguments, I examine the manner in which an auteur not only shapes his or her biography, but also establishes distinct personas to appeal to different audiences. It will also shed light on Kevin Smith himself, as fascinating and contradictory a figure as one can find in the contemporary film industry.

As the invocation of the term 'auteur' will, almost without fail, polemicize a reader with even a glancing knowledge of the history of film criticism, it is perhaps necessary to qualify the use of the term as it applies to the subject matter at hand. Andrew Sarris, though much criticized (and rightly so) in current circles, introduced some facets of auteur criticism that those approaching cinema with a director-centric mindset still return to. In *The American Cinema*, Sarris posits, "The auteur critic is obsessed with the wholeness of the art and the artist. He looks at a film as a whole, a director as a whole. The parts, however entertaining individually, must cohere meaningfully" (Sarris 1968, 30). This thesis, in addition to examining the coherence (and occasional incoherence) between Smith and his films, seeks to examine the reactions of the kinds of "auteur critics" referenced by Sarris. Mainstream critics are still very much under the sway of Sarris' auteurism, and are just as obsessed with divining a 'wholeness' between art and artist. This book explores what happens to the critical response to an artist and his art both when that wholeness is found and when it is not.

For the purposes of this work, Smith's actual position of 'authorship' as evidenced through stylistic and thematic threads that run throughout his work is largely irrelevant. For example, one can find an emphasis on male pairings in each of Smith's five films. An exploration of the tenets of the homosocial bond is implicit in most of Smith's work, and *Chasing Amy*, *Dogma* and *Jay and Silent Bob Strike Back* explore the boundaries between the homosocial and the homosexual in the pairings of their characters, to varying degrees. Attributing these and other 'authorial stamps' to Kevin Smith alone is a methodologically and ideologically suspect move, however, as key texts by theorists Foucault, Barthes and Wollen highlighted in the 1960s and 70s (Gunning, 3). Smith, though acting as the writer, director, and often editor of his films, certainly does not work without collaboration from actors, producers and technicians, many of whom have worked with him on multiple projects. He is also obviously not immune to the influence of the film industry. In short, if a viewer is inclined to approach Smith's films looking for an auteur in a traditional sense, he or she can certainly find one. The converse is also true.

What this paper will concern itself with, however, is the construction of *the idea* of Kevin Smith's authorship by a number of forces. Mainstream critics began viewing Smith as an auteur after the debut of *Clerks*, partly for a number of reasons that will be detailed below, but partly because mainstream critics are, as noted above, still much enamored with the idea of the romantic artist. Smith, too, sees himself as an auteur, as is reflected in his public discourse regarding both his films and himself. Largely as a result of that discourse, Smith's fans view him as an auteur. These three entities—film critics, Kevin Smith fans and Kevin Smith himself—work through extratextual[1] spaces to produce the authorial identity attributed to 'Kevin Smith.' As the writer/director of the texts at the center of said identity, Smith can use, to some degree, the filmic texts themselves as such a space. Smith, though, often uses the filmic texts to enter into dialogue with critics and/or fans. In the case of Kevin Smith, then, the interplay between the institutions of the critical establishment, fandom, and the filmmaker form an interdependent relationship, each constantly taking another as the frame of reference upon which to construct Smith's authorship. The three are not in constant dialogue with each other, though, for reasons that will be detailed below, and thus there are multiple authorial identities, or 'biographies,' attributed to Smith. This approach is not new, having been used to great effect in Barbara Klinger's study of the reception of the films of Douglas Sirk, *Melodrama and Meaning*. In the introduction, she writes:

> I examine the process of 'reputation building' that took place in relation to Sirk; that is, how his creative identity and the meaning of his melodramas were *constructed* by such factors as his publicized intentions, the practices of critical institutions, the media, and social and political circumstances. Departing from the idea that works alone reveal the genius of the authors, this approach helps us to grasp the dialogic relation between artistic reputations and history—the dynamic circumstances under which an author's status and the status of her or his works are established, sustained, transformed, unappreciated, or even vilified. (Klinger, xiii).

This study of Smith's public personas will attempt a similar, dialogical deconstruction of the factors leading to the creation of his 'biographies.'

The notion of an author's 'biography'—which is less a reflection of actual events in his or her life than of said author's assertions of biography as they relate to the author's work—originates with Russian literary theorist Boris Tomasevskij. "...The biography that is useful to the literary historian is not the author's curriculum vitae," he writes. "What the literary historian really needs is the biographical legend created by the author himself." A 'biographical legend' created by an author is, according to Tomasevskij, "tightly bound to...his work" (Tomasevskij 55). To 'his work,' we can obviously add material circulated not only by the author, but, in the case of contemporary American filmmakers, the press machine that permeates popular culture. This would include press releases, comments about the filmmakers by authors and/or contemporaries, and, of course, by reviewers. The Tomasevskij approach to divining an author's biography has been appropriated by film academics studying directors as well. David Bordwell and Robert Kapsis employ the strategy (to varying degrees) in their respective studies of Carl-Theodor Dreyer and Alfred Hitchcock. As Kapsis notes in his introduction, "one reason the biographical legend or public reputation of a filmmaker...is important to the film historian is that it can influence how viewers derive meaning from a given film" (Kapsis 11). In an age of ever-increasing media saturation and public knowledge of the lives and personalities of filmmakers, the influence of filmmakers' public image on the reception and perception of their work proves highly significant.

Crucial to defining the biography that forms around a modern filmmaker is examining the interviews and publicity that the filmmaker participates in to promote his or her work. As Timothy Corrigan points out, modern American auteurs are "defined by their commercial status and their ability to promote a film," for "in today's commerce we want to know what our authors and auteurs look like or how they act" (Corrigan 43). Corrigan asserts that this is largely accomplished through the interview, "which is one of the few extratextual spaces that can be documented where the auteur, in addressing fans and critical viewers, engages and disperses his or her own organizing agency as an auteur" (Corrigan 52). This thesis will demonstrate that the methods of addressing 'critical viewers' can be quite different than those employed when addressing 'fans.' As a result, an auteur can acquire more than one biography. This can be seen quite clearly in Kevin Smith, whose critical and fanboy biographies are distinct and, at times, at odds with each other.

My recounting of Smith's creation of the fanboy biography aims to examine the ways in which fan culture can be manipulated by one who is well versed in its intricacies. As academic writings on fans and fandom are relatively few in number, it would perhaps be beneficial to define the term and briefly explore the existing research and theories. The concept of the 'fan' is most often thought of in terms of an activity on the part of the 'fannish' individual in question. For example, Henry Jenkins has examined the production of fan fiction and art, while many others have stressed the importance of formal gatherings of fans, namely the convention, or 'con.' Researchers C. Lee Harrington and Denise Bielby, though, point out that "this conceptualization of fan as doer obscures an important dimension of fanship, the acceptance and maintenance of a fan identity. One can do a fan activity without being a fan, and vice versa" (Harrington, 86).

Fandom is a term used to describe a large, diverse community of fans. Most often the term carries the connotation of media fans, or, more specifically, sci-fi/fantasy fans. The term can also be applied to specific groups within the whole of fandom, i.e. *Star Trek* fandom or comic book fandom. The types of fans who are more likely to be associated with fandom are often stigmatized and marginalized, especially in contrast to the more mainstream idea of the sports fan. According to Harrington and Bielby, "Media fans are particularly subject to marginalization because their pleasure derives from fictional narratives rather than from something 'real,' like a basketball game" (Harrington, 4). The stigmatizing attitudes regarding fandom are instrumental, however, in fostering a subcultural sense of community among its adherents. In many ways, the less respected a genre or medium is by the mainstream, the stronger the communal bonds forged between its fans become.

The above definition and description of fandom demonstrate that being a part of a fan community (or multiple ones) is different from being what is more commonly construed as a 'fan'. To again turn to a sports analogy, one may be a 'fan' of a professional football team, but may not be the type to memorize the entire team's statistics and paint one's face at the game. The latter is more akin to fandom. In fandom, there is a deeper engagement of the subject matter, and a sense of community is shared with others who engage the material at that level. The 'fan' in the sense of the sports analogy is more akin to a 'viewer' of media. The viewer may enjoy the subject matter, but he or she is unlikely to be engaging it and creating an identity around it as a fan might.

There is also, it should be noted, an economic factor that can be used to divide viewers from members of a fandom. Fandom members are much more likely to spend significant amounts of money on merchandise connected to the subject matter. Conversely, the producers of the media around which a fandom has arisen often profit from (or, to be more cynical, exploit) the obsessive, completist behaviors often found in members of a fandom by producing a wide variety of merchandise aimed directly at fandom's wallet.

Much of the writing on fandom is focused purely on the audience, examining the manner in which an active fan community interacts with a text, often ascribing a utopian, democratic quality to the process. Henry Jenkins accordingly devotes much of his book *Textual Poachers* to examining the fan-produced text, in the forms of fan fiction and fan art. When Jenkins and others examine the producers of the texts around which a fandom has, it is generally to note the ways in which they try to usurp the right to interpret the text from the fans. Jenkins relates a story in which *Star Trek* creator Gene Roddenberry, upset by fans' interpretations of the show, organized a 'fan liaison' to inform fans of the 'correct' interpretation, thereby attempting a negation, in Jenkins' eyes, of the fan engagement with the text (Harrington, 157). In reality, though, producers of fan-oriented media can and often do consciously manipulate the texts to appeal to tendencies unique to fandom. Kevin Smith, in some respects, is unique, as he very obviously has risen out of the rank and file of fandom to become one of its biggest stars. One could thus assert that his success is just the extreme case of fan-produced text. Indeed, this is how many in the fan community approach his work. On the other hand, he uses many of the same subtle techniques for shaping fan response that a figure like George Lucas employs. As fandom will be herein discussed as an institution, often compared and contrasted with journalistic film criticism, it would be prudent to point out the inherently informal nature of fan communities. When arguments are made that begin 'Kevin Smith fandom reacted by...' or 'This prompted X reaction among Smith fans,' it should be borne in mind that fandom is an amorphous, often contradictory entity. In this, it is akin to Klinger's discussion of 'mass camp' reactions to Douglas Sirk's films in *Melodrama and Meaning* (Klinger, 132-56). One can speak of general trends in fandom as it approaches Kevin Smith, but this is not to say that he prompts a monolithic response from it.

The divide between the traditional notions of 'fans'/viewers and fandoms noted earlier should be kept in mind when examining the fandom that has formed around Kevin Smith. While it is true that many directors have 'fans,' this generally implies only that the media consumer in question follows a filmmaker's work. Perhaps the 'fan' may seek out interviews with the director, own the films on DVD, or may purchase a critical study or biography of the director. These directors (and their films), though, provide little solid ground upon which the foundations of fandom—obsessiveness and/or community building—could be built. Kevin Smith is one of the few directors (outside of the science fiction/fantasy/horror axis) around whom a genuine fandom has coalesced, for reasons that will be detailed below.

The Creation of the Author(s)

Kevin Smith's debut film, *Clerks* (Miramax, 1994), had its first public screening on October 3, 1993 at the Independent Feature Film Market (IFFM), a marketplace for independent films held annually in New York City. The IFFM is/was designed as a way for members of the Independent Feature Project[2] to present their films to potential buyers, festival programmers, agents and the like. Independent filmmakers' representative John Pierson is not kind in describing the IFFM in its '90s incarnation. In his book *Spike, Mike, Slackers & Dykes*, he refers to the market as "an undistinguished mass of unreleaseable films...a toxic dump" (Pierson, 37). Critic Amy Taubin, covering the IFFM for the *Village Voice*, was more diplomatic in describing the 1993 event, writing, "Only a handful of filmmakers achieve their cherished goals: a slot at the Sundance or the Berlin film festivals, a nod from Fine Line or Miramax. It's just as unlikely that a buyer will find the film whose box office value will offset the IFFM entry fee [$500] let alone pay the rent for the next year" (Taubin 1993, 66).

Smith had decided that the IFFM was the best place to take *Clerks* based on Taubin's coverage of the 1991 market. Smith expounds upon this in the introduction to the published *Clerks* screenplay, writing,

> ...I was pupil-deep in the cinema listings [of the *Village Voice*] when I saw a photo of a guy, not that much older looking than myself, being profiled in an

article—the caption of which read, 'Richard Linklater is the person that IFFM attendees most want to be.' I read on—this chap Linklater had made a movie a year prior, and it was getting high marks from many folks, including the article's author—Amy Taubin …The next morning, I got a frame and placed Amy Taubin's article in it, hanging it near my desk, beside my word processor. It inspired me …When I'd finished *Clerks*, I knew I had to bring it to the IFFM, as per Ms. Taubin's article. (Smith 1997, x)

Smith would later expound upon the influence that seeing Linklater's *Slacker* (Orion Classics, 1991) had upon him, but it is important to remember that it was Taubin's article that first planted the notion of the independent film scene in Smith's head.

Smith's foray into independent film relates a day in the life of two twenty-something clerks, Dante (Brian O'Halloran) and Randall (Jeff Anderson). The two work minimum-wage jobs in a convenience store and an adjacent video store, respectively. Lacking drive and ambition, they concern themselves more with the intricacies of the futuristic *Star Wars* trilogy than the futures awaiting them. Dante is the more reflective of the pair, a trait that only serves to send him into a deep dissatisfaction with his station in life. This malaise manifests itself through Dante's inability to choose between his current girlfriend and an ex-flame. Randall serves as both the film's comic relief and as Satan to the allusively named Dante, gleefully guiding the latter through his minimum-wage hell. Smith appears in the film as the aptly named Silent Bob, who, with his partner Jay (Jason Mewes), is one-half of a drug-dealing duo who loiter outside of the storefronts. Like *Slacker*, *Clerks* is a largely episodic tale of oddball characters and unlikely situations. Unlike *Slacker*, *Clerks* had no obvious visual style with which to woo the critics and/or buyers at the IFFM. Whereas Linklater's film was visually reminiscent of a European cinema (particularly the French New Wave), Smith's film was comprised largely of static two-shots of the protagonists behind the counter, looking almost as if the image had been captured by a ubiquitous security camera.[3]

Fortuitously, it was *Clerks* that Taubin identified as the standout film of the 1993 market. In her coverage of that year's event, she recounted a phone conversation that she had with Smith.

Amy Taubin: (dials a 10-digit New Jersey number while juggling IFFM 264-page catalogue) Is this Kevin Smith?
Kevin Smith: (suspiciously) Yes. Who is this?
Taubin: This is Amy Taubin, I write this film column for the *The Village Voice*, and I heard that your film *Clerks* is really good. Could you send me a cassette?
Smith: Who'd you hear that from? We had a terrible screening. Only 12 people showed up. Is this a crank call?
Taubin: No, this is the real me who was told by one of her most trusted sources, who was told by one of the 12 people at your screening—a Sundance programmer to be exact—that your film is one of the best things at the market.
Smith: Amy Taubin? I have the piece you wrote about Richard Linklater at the 1991 market framed on my wall.

Taubin, in her *Voice* piece, went on to rave about *Clerks*, calling it an "enormously talented first feature" and that the "no-budget 16mm black and white" film was "directed, written and acted with wit and authenticity." Writing about Smith's lack of cinematic aplomb, Taubin commented "it makes absence of style a virtue in its depiction of blue-collar suburban depression and desire" (Taubin 1993, 66). Smith recalls the effect the conversation and Taubin's subsequent article had on him. "I felt validated as an independent filmmaker.

But more important, I felt like I'd been welcomed into the club" (Smith 1997, x). The impact of the review on Smith was obviously confidence boosting, but it had the larger effect of shaping the approach that he would take when discussing the film with journalists and critics.

After the film played at the 1994 Sundance Film Festival (at which it shared the Filmmaker's Trophy) and was picked up for distribution by Miramax, Smith had plenty of opportunities to discuss it. He had become the toast of the indie film scene, and everyone wanted an interview. Not surprisingly, many of the interviews rehash the same information. While this no doubt made for tiring press junkets for Smith, it served to solidify a critical biography by the time the film premiered in theaters in November of 1994.

Before that biography is discussed, it is important to note that certain aspects of Smith's biography would be determined for him by his position in the film industry. Film critics have an automatic desire to ascribe the properties of the auteur to writer/directors, and did so especially in the independent film boom of the early and mid-90s. As Emanuel Levy notes in his book *Cinema of Outsiders*, "The first and most important force driving independent cinema is the need of young filmmakers...to express themselves artistically" (Levy, 21). Roger Ebert, when asked to define independent film, replied, "it's made because it expresses the director's personal vision rather than someone's idea of box-office success" (Levy, 3). In the American independent film in the 1990s, the director is foregrounded and, often, is automatically seen as an artist, just as the makers of 'art cinema' in the 60s and 70s were (Staiger, 181). This is especially true of small-scale, low budget productions (Cook, 271). Such an approach to the independent filmmaker is evident in the way in which Amy Taubin bestowed the aura of artisanship on the style-less visuals of *Clerks*.

The more specific, individual aspects of Smith's auteur persona that Smith had control over the dissemination of, on the other hand, were solidified through numerous interviews and reviews. As most of the press surrounding Smith repeats the same facts over and over, it is perhaps best to examine the cumulative effect of the press. In his 2000 book *Celluloid Mavericks*, a history of American independent film, Greg Merritt relates the facts of *Clerks* thusly: "It was made for $27,000 by a twenty-three-year-old film school dropout from Red Bank, New Jersey. He shot it almost entirely during off-hours in the Quick Stop convenience store where he worked. With money scrounged from his family and credit cards, Kevin Smith wrote, directed and…co-produced his debut" (Merritt, 370). Here we see the major facets of Smith's *Clerks*-era biography laid bare.

Reviewers and journalists would reiterate all or most of these points in each story or review, and almost all would place special emphasis on the autobiographical elements of *Clerks*, second only to the recounting of the film's remarkably low budget. Kenneth Turan of the *Los Angeles Times* referred to the *Clerks* script having been "based on [Smith's] own cool and crazy life behind the counter" (Turan 1994, F1). The *Village Voice*'s J. Hoberman stated, "Smith was actually employed behind the counter of the bunkerlike 7-Elevenoid where the movie unfolds" (Hoberman, 57). Roger Ebert, in making a common comparison to Quentin Tarantino's biography, wrote, "Quentin Tarantino has become famous as a video store clerk who watched all the movies in his store, and then went out and directed *Reservoir Dogs* and *Pulp Fiction*. Kevin Smith has done him one better, by working behind the counter and then making a movie about the store itself" (Ebert 1994, 23). As John Pierson noted, "*Clerks* delivered on its own merits, [but] Kevin's modest 'I worked in that convenience store and plan to be back there for my shift next Monday' backstory didn't hurt" (Pierson, 294).

The other major facet of Smith's biography that was solidified before the release of *Clerks* is the vulgarity of his written dialogue. Though it was mentioned in some of the Sundance press surrounding the film, the ribald language of *Clerks* was not emphasized until the MPAA branded the film with an NC-17 rating upon review. Miramax panicked, and understandably so—they had paid $250,000 for the film and were now faced with the threat of being unable to market it (Smith "Register Dogs", 51). An appeal to the MPAA was mounted, headed by high-profile lawyer Alan Dershowitz (who was working with the O.J. Simpson defense team at the time). Critics, too, rallied to Smith's defense. Bruce Williamson of *Playboy* said of the dialogue, "It's meant to be outrageous. I didn't see anything wrong with it." He and other film journalists signed a petition to the MPAA. The appeal worked, and, without mandating any changes, the MPAA reduced the NC-17 rating to an R (Oldenburg, 6D). The entire saga of the film's rating was covered by both trade and mainstream press, helping to make the relatively unknown director a known commodity in the process.

This controversy, aside from adding another facet to Smith's critical biography and raising his profile, also served to further position Smith as and outsider and a maverick against the system, a label that, as noted, is inherent in the mainstream critical approach to independent filmmakers. Turan went as far as to compare Smith to the most iconoclastic of vulgarians. "Lenny Bruce would have loved 'Clerks,'" he wrote, going on to call the film "rude, boisterous, obscene and irreverently funny" (Turan, 1). The vulgarity controversy reinforced the conception of Smith-as-auteur in the eyes of critics.

Such public controversy also likely helped the box office of *Clerks*. The $27,000 film went on to gross $2.5 million domestically and did healthy business on video (Pierson, 213). The high financial return of the film made Smith all the more visible. Even those who had not seen the film were likely to be aware of him, due to the underdog success story that had built up around him.

John Pierson, conscious of the fact that Smith was independent films' current 'golden boy,' and having befriended Smith while negotiating the *Clerks* deal with Miramax, collaborated with Smith in the book he wrote on the independent film scene, *Spike, Mike, Slackers & Dykes* (published by a Miramax subsidiary). While in production on his second film, Smith participated in "dialogue" sessions with Pierson. Smith acts as "the voice of 'the filmmaker'" in the book, in which conversations between the author and 'the filmmaker' divide the chapters (Pierson, 2). In the book, Smith relates his opinions on independent films of the last decade. Through Pierson, he relates his influences, his likes and his dislikes. He also gets in a few shots at filmmakers whom he finds untalented, notably Rob Weiss (*Amongst Friends* (Fine Line, 1993)). In the end, Smith comes across as exactly what Pierson intended him to be—the 'voice of the filmmaker.' Smith has assumed a position of authority in the independent film scene.

This position would be reiterated in an interview published in *Film History*. Conducted one week before the premiere of Smith's sophomore film, *Mallrats*, Smith slammed film schools for emphasizing theory over filmmaking skills, and then dismisses filmmaking skills in favor of scriptwriting talent. "If you want to write and be a writer/director, either you can write or you can't write. And if you can write, nine times out of ten you can direct" (Duritz, 240). Smith also takes time to question the value of film theory. Making a rare allusion to a semester spent at the Vancouver Film School, Smith commented on their theory classes, remarking, "It was a matter of somebody else giving you their idea of what the movie was about…The only one you could ever listen to is the filmmaker himself. You produce the filmmaker and let him tell me what it's about and I'll believe him! But you've got a teacher…translating what this film was, it just doesn't wash" (Duritz, 239). Smith here takes a very authoritative tone in discussing independent filmmaking, obviously relishing his role as Pierson's 'voice of the filmmaker.' When discussing what constitutes 'independent film,' Smith comes across as particularly opinionated.

The year we were out on the festival circuit, at Sundance, there was a movie like us. There was *Clerks* and there was a movie called *Suture* (1993)...It was a first time film, shot in 35 mm black and white; Luscious! And it's 3.25, wide screen, with actual stars. It cost one million to make. And then there was *Clerks*. And *Clerks* was scrappy, nobody's in it and it was made for twenty-seven grand. You've heard of *Clerks* but you haven't heard of *Suture*. Why is that? That movie looked polished, it looked good...And then ours, which is really down and dirty, is everywhere. So what works, and what doesn't?...Then you have something like *Brothers McMullen* (1995): down and dirty made but no edge whatsoever! It's just like every mainstream romance comedy you've ever seen and it makes ten million. And because it doesn't look as good as any other Hollywood movies, people will assume 'that's independent film.' And who's to say that it's not?

Smith quickly answers his own question, stating flatly, "But I'll sit here and I'll decry it 'till the day I die that it is not an independent movie. It's a Hollywood movie without the budget" (Duritz, 243).

But exactly what sort of 'voice' did critics and film aficionados see in this filmmaker? In approaching a filmmaker with the biographical legend that has thus far coalesced around Smith, I would argue that most critics saw in Kevin Smith a neo-John Waters. J. Hoberman explicitly compared *Clerks* to early John Waters films, and it is not farfetched to think that critics would have noted the similarities in the personas of each (Pierson, 22). The two share many biographical facets, extending beyond their status as 'independents.' Like Waters, Smith had become a 'name' by producing, writing and directing an ultra low-budget feature that was best known for its vulgarity—*Clerks* was Smith's *Pink Flamingos* (New Line, 1972). Visually, both Waters' film and *Clerks* are amateurish, each revealing its low-budget origins. In both cases, critics saw this as a virtue. Both filmmakers also closely identify themselves and their work with their hometowns. North Jersey is just as crucial an aspect of *Clerks* as Baltimore is to the oeuvre of Waters. Actors drawn almost exclusively from the directors' groups of friends populate the films of each. In fact, Pierson, writing in *Spike, Mike, Slackers & Dykes*, notes that

> Waters probably set more independent standards than anyone would think. He had an attitude/vision, which he got on screen through primitive means with virtually no money by assembling a support group in his home town and capitalizing on their meager talents through a combination of charm and shock value" (Pierson, 11).

Without the opening sentence, Pierson could have easily been describing Smith, so similar are their critical biographies.

On a less superficial level, though, Smith also echoes Waters in the primacy his films give to a disenfranchised youth culture. Waters' characters are all, for lack of a better term, freaks. Transsexuals, the clinically insane, drag queens, junkies, and serial killers populate his films (both in characters and in performers). They represented the far fringes of culture in a time when hippies, a supposed fringe culture, were much less subversive than they seemed. Smith, by contrast, populated *Clerks* with somewhat-stereotypical Gen-X characters, but still managed to capture a sense of white male disenfranchisement and societal despair, especially in the character of Dante.[4] While the differences in these representations of disenfranchisement are certainly extreme (and the social critiques leveled by *Clerks* nowhere near as damning as Waters'), critics did, it seems, cast Smith in a similar 'outsider' mold.

Ultimately, though critics embraced Smith as a Watersesque subculture iconoclast, Smith's own ideas about the direction of his career would take him in a different direction—one that clashed with the biographical preconceptions with which critics were primed to approach his work.

Before the publication of either *Spike, Mike, Slackers & Dykes* or the *Film History* interview, Smith's second film, *Mallrats* (Gramercy, 1995) was released in theaters on October 20, 1995. Smith had been contracted to do a follow-up film for Universal under producer Jim Jacks. The film was set up at Gramercy Pictures, Universal's 'boutique' label, handled much of the larger studio's independent and niche films. Jacks' original idea was to have Smith remake *Clerks*, but the widespread awareness of the film made that idea unfeasible. Instead, Jacks enjoined Smith to write a similar film (*Clerks* DVD commentary). Smith related the advice to Pierson, saying, "The studio tells me, basically you've had your hip, inside movie and it's done really well for you...But now imagine opening that up. If you're going to make a film, why not have it seen by the broadest, widest possible audience, as opposed to people that are going to be hip and inside? And in terms of thinking about making a studio film, it makes perfect sense. Now this last draft of *Mallrats* plays to me like an *Animal House*" (Pierson, 182).

The studio, though, had a different film in mind when producing *Mallrats*. "What they wanted," Smith relates on the *Mallrats* DVD, "was a smart *Porky's* (1981)...They hadn't had any teen titty films in years. They were talking about how...exhibitors wanted movies with tits. We were being told by the higher-ups: 'We need movies with tits'" (*Mallrats* DVD commentary).

Mallrats abandons the largely episodic format of *Clerks* and attempts a more plot-driven structure. It tells the story of Brodie Bruce (Jason Lee) and T.S. Quint (Jeremy London), two college-age slackers dumped by their respective girlfriends on the same morning. The two seek solace at the local mall, only to find that they cannot escape their romantic troubles so easily. Like *Clerks*, the film is heavy on dialogue. Smith does blend some slapstick comedy and some action scenes into the mix, and, in accordance with Universal's wishes, involves his characters in sexual hi-jinks as well. Unfortunately, films like *American Pie* (Universal, 1999) and *Road Trip* (Dreamworks SKG, 2000) had not yet revived the teen sex comedy as a viable genre. *Mallrats* flopped at the box office, recapping only $2.12 million of its $6.1 million budget. Critics, like theatergoers, roundly rejected the film.[5] Despite a few moderately good reviews (notably from the *Village Voice, Variety* and *Entertainment Weekly*), the movie was harshly attacked by most critics. There is widespread rejection of the vulgarity and lowbrow sexual humor in the film (the same sort of humor that critics defended in the MPAA petition). A few mention the film's admittedly glaring technical flaws and cinematic deficiencies. Many of the criticisms, though, are nearly exclusively focused on Smith himself. One of the more representative reviews comes from Kenneth Turan. His prior praise of *Clerks* makes his negative review of *Mallrats* all the more damning. The first line of the review states, "If the Sundance Institute or the AFI ever offers a course advising directors of successful first films what to avoid the second time around, *Mallrats* could be at the heart of the curriculum." He ends the review by noting, "When this film ends with the on-screen notice that 'Jay and Silent Bob will return in *Chasing Amy*,' it feels more like a warning than a prediction" (Turan, 1995, F2).

Ebert closed his review with this statement: "The year that *Clerks* played at the Cannes Film Festival, I was the chairman of a panel discussion of independent filmmakers. Most of them talked about their battles to stay free from Hollywood's playsafe strategies. But Kevin Smith cheerfully said he'd be happy to do whatever the studios wanted, if they'd pay for his films. At the time, I thought he was joking." Smith had, in the eyes of Ebert (and many critics), betrayed his independent film roots. As Ebert noted, "*Clerks* spoke with the sure, clear voice of an original filmmaker. In *Mallrats* the voice is muffled, and we sense instead advice from the tired, the establishment, the timid and other familiar Hollywood executive types" (Ebert 1995, 45). With *Mallrats*, Smith's artistic authorship in the eyes of critics had been lost. This is probably due, at least in part, to the fact that *Mallrats* was a studio-financed film, thus severing the link between Smith and the 'independent outsider' archetype, as Ebert's review posits. Smith had failed to live up to the John Waters mold in which critics had viewed him. As far as the critics could see, there was no personal voice in *Mallrats*. On the contrary, though, a strongly personal voice can be heard in *Mallrats*. However, it does not speak a language that most critics can hear. Smith had alluded to as much in the aforementioned *Film History* interview, saying "With *Mallrats*, the dialogue speaks to a very specific audience [whereas] *Clerks* spoke to a much broader audience" (Duritz, 246).

Despite being written off as a one-hit wonder by many critics, it was after the release and failure of *Mallrats* that Kevin Smith's biographical legend began to diversify. Where *Clerks* had cast him in the role of low-budget filmmaker/artist with a finger on the pop-culture pulse, *Mallrats* shaped a new persona for Smith—that of 'fanboy.'[6]

'Fanboy' is a term used within the milieu of comic book readers. Defined by Matthew Pustz in his book *Comic Book Culture*, fanboys are "comic book readers who take what they read too seriously" (Pustz, 71). Pustz notes, however, that many comics fans and creators use the term with pride. He notes a degree of fun that is had by those who "may obsess over minor details...For them, being a fanboy or acting fanboyish involves a certain degree of irrationality, especially in regard to choosing favorite characters or comics based not on aesthetic criteria but rather on some gut-level determination of 'coolness'" (Pustz, 76).

Those who watched *Mallrats* are not likely to have become fans based on any 'aesthetic criteria.' However, as Kevin Smith noted, "it seemed to find its audience on video" (*Mallrats*

DVD). "Believe me, I don't think it's our strongest work," he wrote on an Internet forum. "But there are tons of folk who feel (strongly) that it's the best thing we've ever done" (*Psycomic* website forum). It is a fanboy mentality that Smith tapped into with *Mallrats* that initially led to the establishment of a fan base.

In *Mallrats* Smith reveals himself to be a comic book fanboy of the highest order, and by doing so, primes a potential fan base to approach his work in a fanboy-esque manner. He accomplishes this through references to comic books, having a protagonist who is the embodiment of the fanboy and by appropriating the comic book notion of continuity in *Mallrats*.

It should be pointed out that, while a pre-existing comic book fandom is certainly tapped into by *Mallrats*, the film also appeals to potential fans unaccustomed to the comic book conventions described below. The methods by which the film achieves this, though, can be seen to parallel the methods by which comics have traditionally built and maintained a fanbase. Smith, then, uses the techniques of comic book fandom to appeal to both comic book fans as well as those who have no connections to comics.

The groundwork for the establishment of the fanboy persona was laid in *Clerks*. Though the film has no specific references to comic books[7], there is a understanding of fandom implicit in the way in which Randall and Dante debate the minutiae of the *Star Wars* (1977) trilogy. This scene, in which the pair discuss the morality of the destruction of the Death Star, became celebrated among *Star Wars* fans, as evidenced by its inclusion in the May 1999 special issue of *Premiere* devoted to *Star Wars*. The inclusion of such material in *Clerks* no doubt planted the seeds of a fan base, as many comic book fans are also science fiction and movie fans. As Henry Jenkins notes in his fan-culture analysis *Textual Poachers*, "Media fan culture...may be understood not in terms of an exclusive interest in any one series or genre; rather, media fans take pleasure in making intertextual connections across a broad range of media texts" (Jenkins 1992, 36). Such overlap between comics fandom and movie fandom is evident when examining the approach to Smith in prominent media fan outlets. *Ain't-It-Cool News*, a popular film website run by self-avowed 'geek' Harry Knowles, pays close attention to Smith's upcoming film projects, though the 'talkbacks' on the site (in which readers share their opinions of the news items and rumors) invariably contain discussions of which comic book films Smith should write and/or direct.

The differences between comic book fandom and a more general media fandom merit discussion, however. Whereas Jenkins notes that fandom generally forms only around less successful television series, comic book fandom as defined and discussed by Pustz revolves around the medium as a whole (Jenkins 1992, 89). Fans certainly have favorite comic book titles, but it is their devotion to the medium that binds them, rather than their devotion to a series. Perhaps this is due to the fact that comics are less successful as a medium, both financially and as a factor within the popular culture (Pustz, 208). Whereas a *Star Trek* fan base may coalesce about the series due to its limited appeal in relation to other television shows, a comic book fan base may be solidified through the limited appeal of the entire medium. This difference between fandoms within more mainstream media and comic book fandom is significant in discussing Smith's use of comic book representational conventions to create a fanbase, and thus much of the argument that follows will focus on a comic fandom as opposed to a more general media fandom. Later, as will be explored, Smith would embrace techniques common to other realms of fandom. *Mallrats*, though, is primarily and resolutely concerned with comics.

The most basic method by which Smith ingratiates himself with comic book fans is by referencing specific comic books, characters and creators in the diegesis of the film. Smith himself refers to *Mallrats* as being "lousy with comic references (lousy meaning lots, not unskilled use of)" (*Mallrats* website).

For example, the opening credits are comprised of fake comic book covers featuring the film's characters. Many of these are puerile parodies of actual comic books, i.e. Buttman (in which the artwork and design style mimic a Batman comic) and The Fantastic Two (modeled after the *Fantastic Four* logo and layout). As these opening credits flash on the screen, a comic book savvy viewer is already treated to a multitude of in-jokes, an easy way to appeal to comic fans (Pustz, 211).

Throughout the film, imagery from comic books dominates the frame. Spider-Man posters cover walls; references are made to the proper storage and handling of comics. The name of the main character, Brodie Bruce, recalls the tendency for comic book characters to have alliterative names: Clark Kent, Lois Lane, Lex Luthor, Peter Parker, Bruce Banner, etc. Smith himself, returning as Silent Bob, dons a Batman-like helmet at one point in the film and is revealed to have a utility belt and grappling gun identical to those used in the 1989 *Batman* film. Upon being rescued by Silent Bob and his superhero gear, Jay is even prompted to appropriate one of Jack Nicholson's lines from that film. "Where do you get those wonderful toys?" he asks of his partner.

To the fanboy, perhaps the most significant nod to comic book culture is the cameo by legendary comic book creator Stan Lee (Figure 1). Lee, co-creator of such comic properties as Spider-Man, the Hulk and the X-Men, is approached by Brodie for romantic advice and harassed for his inside knowledge of superhero trivia. Smith notes on the *Mallrats* DVD that Universal felt that Lee's cameo was reminiscent of Wolfman Jack in George Lucas's *American Graffiti*. These cameos however, function in markedly different ways. Whereas Wolfman Jack, a famous 1950s deejay, was a noted and prominent figure in American popular culture, indelibly linked with rock and roll, Stan Lee exists as a prominent figure only within the comic book subculture. Where Wolfman Jack served to heighten the sense of nostalgia in *American Graffiti* for the mass Baby Boomer audience, the inclusion of Stan Lee as a figure to be awed and revered (as he is in *Mallrats*) serves to validate the film for a small niche of viewers. In this respect, the Lee cameo is much closer to that of the punk band The Ramones in *Rock and Roll High School* (New World, 1979), a movie that has become a cult film largely due to its inclusion of a cult band.

Figure 1: Fanboy reverence for Stan Lee

Mallrats speaks to a comic-minded audience through its protagonist as well. The character of Brodie, as played by Jason Lee, is both the quintessential fanboy and a fanboy's idealized self.[8] As the quintessential fanboy, Brodie is shown to have a 'vault' in which he keeps his comics, and which he warns his friend T.S. not to touch. Brodie refers to a merchant selling comics at a local flea market as a 'savage' for not storing the comics with protective backing boards. Obsessive care of one's collection is a common characteristic of many comic book fans (Pustz, 215).

Brodie also 'takes what he reads too seriously,' to quote Pustz, as demonstrated by the scene in which he goes to great lengths to explain to T.S. the disastrous biological implications of the sex life of Superman and Lois Lane. He also questions Stan Lee on the superhuman attributes of superhero genitalia. Such debate over minutiae (particularly as it relates to issues that could never be raised in mainstream comics) is rampant in fanboy culture (Pustz, 70). In short, comic book-minded viewers of *Mallrats* were and are likely to see some of their own fanboyish tendencies in the character of Brodie. These types of debates are also found in a more general media fandom as well, as Jenkins notes in relation to *Twin Peaks* fans (Jenkins 1995, 77), and as Will Brooker sees in the Internet dialogues about *Blade Runner* (Warner Bros., 1982), *Star Wars* and *Alien* (20th Century Fox, 1979) fans (Brooker, 50).

Brodie, however, seems more well rounded than the stereotypical fanboy. Pustz refers to the extreme negative fanboy stereotype as being "overweight, slovenly, lazy…[one who] lacks interpersonal skills…his sexual activity is limited to daily masturbation" (Pustz, 72). Brodie, in contrast, is trim and handsome (if a bit unkempt), has an attractive girlfriend (with whom he has sex in the mall elevator) and is presented as the most popular character in the film. Everyone seems to know and like Brodie, from drug dealers to preppy high school girls. Brodie even antagonizes other comic readers in the course of the film, going so far as to physically attack a surly comic shop owner and verbally berating the owner's assistant, yelling, "Fuck you, fanboy!" The surly comic shop owner is one of the most persistent stereotypes within comic book culture, and Brodie's attack probably serves as an in-joke for fans as much as it serves to idealize him as dynamic and active.

Not having Brodie conform strictly to the fanboy stereotype serves two functions. First, it allows real-life fanboys (whether they exemplify the stereotype or not) to see him as an ideal. Brodie's character is both an unrepentant fanboy and 'the coolest kid in the mall,' so to speak, contradicting the "bad reputation" comic reading carries with it (Pustz, 208). Second, Brodie's well-rounded nature serves to make him accessible to a mainstream viewer. It should be remembered that Smith's mandate from Universal was to make his film accessible to "the widest possible audience" (*Mallrats* DVD).

Presenting Brodie as a full-blown comic fan with any or all of the negative stereotypical trappings would have led to a character more ripe for ridicule than identification (i.e., the 'Comic Book Guy' of *The Simpsons*). Smith would comment in 2001, "In my movies, I've always referenced comic book culture and never painted it as geek culture" (McLaughlin "Hollywood Heat", 44). Nowhere in his filmography is this more true than in the character of Brodie.

The third and arguably most important manner in which Smith both identifies himself as a fanboy and inspires the same in an audience is through the use of continuity. Whereas continuity in terms of filmmaking refers to keeping the details of set, costume, makeup etc. constant from shot to shot, continuity in the comic book sense of the word implies something much broader. Defined by Pustz, continuity is "the intertextuality that links stories in the minds of the creators and readers." The main facet of continuity as it applies to Smith's films is the idea of "an established chronology" in a "coherent universe" bridging multiple texts (Pustz, 129). Smith refers to comic book continuity as "an idea that always appealed to me, and it was something I wanted to establish in the films that I made" (*Mallrats* website).

The groundwork for the use of continuity had been laid in *Clerks*, as much time is spent by Dante and Randall discussing characters, locations and situations that are never seen. In *Clerks*, much of the discussion revolved around high school friends and events, giving the viewer a clear sense that the pair had not moved past their adolescence. Ultimately, though, this random name-dropping served to give the viewer the impression that the world of the characters was much larger than the static two-shot of the store counter presented by the film. Additionally, reusing the names of characters that never appear onscreen is the type of minutiae that breeds obsessive revisitation of a text—a staple of fandom.

In the opening scene of *Mallrats*, T.S.' girlfriend Brandi relates a convoluted story in which one of her friends, Julie

Dwyer, died the previous day in the YMCA pool while doing laps. This death prevents Brandi from accompanying T.S. to Florida and is thus the impetus for the story. Astute viewers of *Clerks*, though, will remember that Julie Dwyer is the ex-girlfriend of Dante whose coffin Randal knocks over in the funeral home. *Mallrats*, consequently, takes place in the same 'world' as *Clerks* and is presumably set a few days before. Smith confirms the chronology on the *Mallrats* DVD, saying "*Mallrats* takes place the day before *Clerks* in the continuity."

Mallrats is rife with references to the intertextuality between itself and *Clerks*. The shared world of the films would become known as the "View Askewniverse," an amalgamation of the name of Smith's production company (View Askew) and the comic book practice of each publisher's comic stories being contained in a separate 'universe.' The foremost of these nods to the Askewniverse is the reappearance of Jay and Silent Bob.

Smith refers to Jay and Silent Bob as "my most popular creations" and Gramercy Pictures' marketing campaign recognized this (*Chasing Amy* DVD liner notes). One of the television ads for *Mallrats* revolved around the duo, heralding "For the first time in color, Jay and Silent Bob" (*Mallrats* DVD). Thus was the intertextuality of *Clerks* and *Mallrats* foregrounded for potential audiences. Indeed, the latter film seems to take prior knowledge of these characters for granted. The first appearance of the two in *Mallrats* seems to be a cause for celebration, as we first see Jay's hand pounding out a beat on a storefront window, a beat that becomes a rock and roll intro for him and Silent Bob, and one over which the two dance. Silent Bob's name is not revealed to the audience until well into the duo's first scene; he is, in fact, first referred to as 'shithead' by Jay—the assumption seems to be that we already know these two. Smith hardly seems to be 'playing it wide' when introducing the pair.

Other characters from *Clerks* are explicitly mentioned by name. Rick Derris, the personal trainer revealed to have slept with Dante's ex-girlfriend in *Clerks*, is referenced as having done the same with an ex of T.S. Some characters in *Mallrats* are hinted at as being related to characters from *Clerks*. Brodie makes reference to his sexually perverse cousin Walter, the name of Randall's cousin in *Clerks* who died while attempting to fellate himself. The question is thus suggested to the continuity-minded viewer—are Randall and Brodie related? A contestant in the *Mallrats*' climactic game show is named Gil Hicks and is played by Brian O'Halloran, the actor who portrayed *Clerks*' Dante Hicks. By including these minor allusions to the intertextuality of the films, Smith prompts the continuity-conscious into the sorts of debates that Brodie revels in. And, in encouraging the viewer to tease out these references, Smith creates a viewer who engages the text on a level unnecessary to the understanding and/or enjoyment of the narrative. He has seeded the type of textual engagement upon which fandoms are built.

Paul Dini, comic writer and co-creator of *Batman: The Animated Series*, in 2001 pointed out what many comic fans had divined years earlier, writing,

> It's no accident that comics legend Stan Lee appeared as a sort of spiritual guide to comics fan Brodie in *Mallrats*. The parallels to the Marvel universe and Smith's own View Askewniverse are very clear. The inhabitants of each world all know each other and interact, with events taking place in one corner affecting the lives of characters in another...Substituting Leonardo, N.J., for Marvel's Manhattan, Kevin Smith has created an environment no less intricate and involving...(Dini, 5)

An appeal to continuity is also the method by which Smith attracts fans that are not versed in comic book culture, for continuity as Smith presents it is just the comic book culture's favorite facet of the 'open narrative.' Open narratives are in no way unique to comics, and are much more widely discussed in terms of television shows, particularly in relation to the most fully realized version of the open narrative, the soap opera. It should be noted, however, that all almost all series television works on this model to a degree.

Several elements distinguish the soap opera from other narrative forms; most notable is its resistance to closure...soaps are characterized by an 'endless middle'; story lines are never finally resolved....open-ended narratives engage viewers through the development of story telling within the text and foster the perception of soap characters as real, with human strengths and limitations (Harrington, 13).

Figure 2: *The Mallrats poster-as-comic book*

Authors Harrington and Bielby go on to point out that open narratives make the "boundaries of the text more difficult to determine," a facet that eases the ability of the would-be fan to immerse him or herself within the text. As noted, this is a matter of degrees within almost all television shows: the more 'open' the narrative (i.e., the more individual episodes interact with each other), the higher the likelihood that a fandom will arise around that show. Examples of primetime shows that feature open narratives and have attracted large fandoms include *The X-Files*, *Buffy the Vampire Slayer* and *Sex in the City*. Smith, then, in allowing his films to 'bleed' into one another by way of shared characters, settings and histories, taps into the fanbase that potentially exists in relation to open narratives.

By making such overt and covert allusions to both comic books and the fanboy culture in *Mallrats*, Smith had thus primed a comic book savvy audience to react to his films in the same manner by which they react to the comic book medium itself. Moreover, by demonstrating that he was literate in what Pustz refers to as the "language" of the fanboy, Smith had made it clear that he was one of them. Thus, though critics missed it entirely, *Mallrats* is actually a very personal film, in that it expresses a love and understanding of a maligned subculture. In 2001, in an interview with a *Star Wars* fan magazine, Smith would be asked,

Interviewer: Your movies are pretty much the only ones that treat fans of comics and sci-fi…
Smith: With a degree of respect…That was the appeal of getting into film for me—wanting to go see something on screen that I could identify with…I do go to comic book shows…I can identify with those characters, their passions, their interests (Chernoff, 12-3).

Smith's rapport with a comic book audience was clear to those responsible for the marketing of the film. The film's original poster was modeled after a comic book cover, going so far as to bearing the Comics Code Authority Stamp of Approval (Figure 2). Trading cards were produced for the film, significant in that the card market is linked to the comic book market, as many comic specialty shops sell collectible cards as well as comics. Ads for the film appeared in comic books, highlighting the cameo by Stan Lee and bearing a stamp of approval by *Wizard* Magazine (the preeminent comic publication) praising *Mallrats* as "The best comic book film ever!" Gramercy sponsored a contest in which the winner would attend a private screening of *Mallrats* and meet the artist of Spider-Man (Morrison and Millar, 21). While these efforts were not enough to bring many comic fans into the theaters, it is not farfetched to think that said promotional efforts might share some of the responsibility for the film's subsequent success on video.

Smith's fanboy persona suggested by *Mallrats*, it should be noted, had not yet developed into a full-fledged 'biography' in Tomasevskij's sense of the word. No reviews or interviews regarding *Mallrats* had added anything to Smith's biography that pertains specifically to the fanboy persona. This would change following his next film, *Chasing Amy*.

Chasing Amy and the Integration/Division of Smith's Personas

Clerks had established Kevin Smith as a truly independent auteur who made a small, semi-autobiographical film and became an against-all-odds success story. *Mallrats* prompted most critics to revise their impression of Smith; most saw him as a one-note purveyor of juvenile humor. In the absence of critical praise, however, a new persona arose, one that was imperceptible to most viewers. A comic book savvy fanboy persona drew like-minded fans to Smith. With this dichotomy in place, Smith moved on to his third film, *Chasing Amy*. Released in the spring of 1997, it would become a critical favorite and a box office success, prompting many critics to hail Smith's return as a filmmaker to be watched. More importantly, the film brings together both of Smith's personas and forces them to compete—artist versus fanboy. The resolution of this conflict in the film, in which the artist triumphs, is at the heart of the critical reappraisal and approval of Smith.

Ostensibly, *Chasing Amy* is the story of a man who falls in love with a lesbian and the tension that the ensuing relationship causes between the man and his best friend. Smith made it clear that this would be the subject of his third film as early as the aforementioned *Film History* interview, in which he noted that he would be returning to his independent roots (Duritz, 246). *Chasing Amy* is also mentioned in a 1995 Amy Taubin piece (in retrospect, rather ominously titled "Before the

Fall") about *Mallrats'* upcoming autumnal release (Taubin 1995, 72).

Chasing Amy stars Ben Affleck, Jason Lee and Joey Lauren Adams, all three of whom had played substantial roles in *Mallrats*. Smith had a favorite line to feed to reporters when giving interviews about *Chasing Amy*. "*Mallrats* was my $6 million casting call for *Chasing Amy*." Elaborating on the necessity of *Mallrats*, Smith said,

It's easy to say now, but I'm a big proponent of a flop movie. Every filmmaker should have to make a flop because it builds character. It's like you quit or you go on, and maybe after one or two mistakes, you'll know never to do that again…I think it was really essential to get that film out of my system (Rea, C7).

Here, Smith seems to be claiming that 'he learned his lesson' from *Mallrats* and 'won't do it again.' This idea would be developed in *Chasing Amy* itself.

Though he emphasized the necessity of the failure of *Mallrats*, Smith took pains to distance *Chasing Amy* from his previous film. While presenting at the 1996 Independent Spirit Awards, the director opened by saying, "I want to take this time to apologize for *Mallrats*. I don't know what I was thinking" (*Mallrats* website). Though Smith would later claim the comment was a joke, critics seized upon this sound bite. Roger Ebert referenced it in his review of *Chasing Amy*, writing, "[Smith] started out with a great movie called *Clerks*, then followed up with a movie that was so bad he apologized for it" (Ebert 1997, 35).

Much of the press and many of the reviews of *Chasing Amy* highlight the fact that the film is based upon events in Smith's real life. Smith had developed a romantic relationship with actress Joey Lauren Adams on the set of *Mallrats* and his initial misgivings about her sexual past were the inspiration for the film's story. The knowledge that the film was based on Smith's personal experiences was so widespread that it prompted *Entertainment Weekly* to ask (and answer) the question, "Did Kevin Smith really date a lesbian?" (Gaines, 87). In this we can see the autobiographical aspect of Smith's critical biography resurface. In regard to Smith's biography circa *Clerks*, critics were arguably most enamored with the parallels between the film and Smith's life.[9] Thus, a return to a more personal mode of storytelling was perhaps the best way to win back critics. In one interview, Smith seemed to place the blame for the failure of *Mallrats* on its lack of autobiographical elements, saying, "When it came time to do the second film, I didn't have much personal to say. If I were going to make a personal movie at the time it would have been about traveling from festival to festival with a first film" (Rea, C7). *Chasing Amy*, in contrast, takes great pains to emphasize the importance of 'having something personal to say,' a recurring phrase in the film.

While critics were certainly positioned to embrace *Chasing Amy*, Smith also took pains to prime his fanboy persona with its corresponding audience. As he had done earlier with *Mallrats*, Smith recruited well-known comic artists to work on the film. Mike Allred, Joe Quesada and Jimmy Palmiotti (prominent comic book writer/artists) all contribute artwork to the film and each has a cameo in the opening sequence.[10]

Said opening sequence takes place at a comic book convention, events that Pustz describes as "holidays" for fans (Pustz, 158). This sequence sets the tone for the world of *Chasing Amy*. All of the principal characters are comic book writers and/or artists. We see characters creating, selling, reading, distributing and discussing comics throughout the film. The comic book fan can find much to identify with in *Chasing Amy*.

The same can be said to be true of the Kevin Smith fan. References to the previous two films are interspersed throughout. *Chasing Amy* establishes itself in the View Askewniverse timeline by having Joey Lauren Adams' character Alyssa Jones refer to Julie Dwyer, her friend who "died in a pool."[11] Alyssa is a character that was first mentioned in *Clerks* by her sister, Heather Jones. Mention is made in *Chasing Amy* of the settings of both *Clerks* (Quick Stop Groceries) and *Mallrats* (Eden Prairie Mall). Continuity is firmly established for the discriminating fan, as evidenced by "the Askewniverse Legend," a map-like guide to the people and places that populate Smith's New Jersey included in the liner notes of the *Chasing Amy* laserdisc and DVD.

The best reactions of both critics and existing fans were thus primed in *Chasing Amy* by presenting viewers of each persuasion with the Kevin Smith they love. Instead of simply invoking each persona to satisfy its respective audience though, Smith brings the two into conflict. This is accomplished in the film's subplot.

The two principal male characters of the film are comic book creators Holden McNeil (Ben Affleck) and Banky Edwards (Jason Lee). After achieving moderate success with a self-published autobiographical comic, the two hit the big time with a superhero comic series, *Bluntman & Chronic*. The wildly popular comic is the talk of the industry, and MTV approaches the two to do a cartoon version of the book. Personal issues divide them, however, and they go their separate ways: Holden returns to the small press with a personal story, while Banky continues to appeal to fans' tastes.

The career arc of Banky and Holden is quite clearly an analogue for the career trajectory of Smith prior to *Chasing Amy*. This is established by a montage that runs under the opening credits. A variety of news articles from both mainstream press and comic industry trade publications relate the history of the duo prior to the first scene of the film.[12] Their first, autobiographical comic is titled *37*, a clear reference to *Clerks*' infamous joke about the number of sexual partners had by Dante's girlfriend. This is established by a sidebar in the entertainment section of an Asbury Park, New Jersey newspaper (Figure 3). The article, upon closer examination, states that Holden and Banky "took their experiences stocking shelves at the Atlantic Highlands Food City and turned them into the newest entry in the growing world of self-published comics." Here, we see the biggest aspect of Smith's *Clerks*-era biography projected on to the principal characters of *Chasing Amy*.

Figure 3: 37 – The self-published comic as a stand-in for the independent film

The growing popularity of *37* is the subject of the next series of articles in the montage. Graduating from the sidebar, the headline of the 'Lifestyles' section of a larger New Jersey paper proclaims "Local Pair Have Drawing Power" and reports that the two continue to "rack up kudos with their indie comic book."

The Sundance and Cannes awards garnered by *Clerks* come quickly to mind. The next publication is *Comic Shop News*, a small industry publication, which details that Holden and Banky have been signed by a major comic book company—the fictional Contender (Figure 4). The panels shown in this article, assumedly from *37*, show a man putting eggs into his mouth. One of the patrons of the Quick Stop in *Clerks* is shown to do the same, further solidifying the link between the small press comic book and Smith's independent debut film. The Contender deal mirrors Smith's agreement to make his follow-up to *Clerks* at Universal.

37 Pair Headed to Contender

Figure 4

This follow-up, represented by Holden and Banky's sophomore effort, is the next to be highlighted in the montage. Titled *Bluntman & Chronic*, the book features a superheroic pair obviously modeled on Silent Bob and Jay, respectively. The cover of *Bluntman & Chronic* #1 (itself featured on the cover of the industry trade publication *Comics Buyers* Guide) makes it clear that the book is an analogue for *Mallrats* (Figure 5). Featured prominently on the cover is LaFours, the Keystone-like mall security guard who served as a foil to Jay and Silent Bob in the previous film. Bluntman's costume is very similar to the Batman-esque costume worn by Silent Bob in *Mallrats*. Chronic is seen in a panel of the comic shouting his battle cry, "Snoochie Boochies!" Jay endlessly spouted such nonsense verse in *Mallrats*.

The final image shown in the montage is Bluntman and Chronic on the cover of *Wizard* magazine, the highest selling comic book magazine on the market (Figure 6). As Pustz notes, "because of its focus on adolescent males, *Wizard* is often considered a fanboy magazine" (Pustz, 178). This references the fanboy-pleasing qualities of *Mallrats*.

Figure 5: Mallrats as a superhero fantasy

The tension for the subplot is thus established during the opening credits—an autobiographical, self-published black and white comic book versus a mainstream color superhero comic book seemingly lacking any real-life grounding. Interestingly, the press surrounding *37* is shown as being in 'legitimate' newspapers while *Bluntman & Chronic* is reported only in comic book outlets. Smith, it could be argued, is commenting on the marginalization of *Mallrats* and its summary dismissal by those in the critical establishment.

Some might contend that the *Mallrats/Bluntman & Chronic* correlation does not account for the fact that, within the world of *Chasing Amy*, the latter is extraordinarily successful. However, the popularity of *Bluntman & Chronic* is only shown in relation to stereotypical fanboys. As Holden comments at one point in the film, "Over- or underweight guys that don't get laid—they're our bread and butter." This is exemplified by one fan, notably played by Ethan Suplee, an actor who (perhaps significantly) played fan-favorite character Willam Black in *Mallrats*. His opinion of *Bluntman & Chronic* (and his thought processes in general) is revealed in his conversation with Holden during the opening comic book convention.

Figure 6: A mock cover of Wizard magazine

Fan: I love this book, man. This shit is awesome! I wish I was like these guys, getting stoned, talking all raw about chicks, fighting supervillains...I love these guys! You know what, they're like Bill and Ted meet...Cheech and Chong!
Holden: I kind of like to think of them as Rosencrantz and Guildenstern meet Vladimir and Estragon.
Fan: Yes! Who?

Here we also meet Holden for the first time. He is thus established as literary, erudite, and totally dismayed with the fan's reaction to *Bluntman and Chronic*. Holden (a name deliberately reminiscent of *The Catcher in the Rye*'s protagonist) represents Smith's independent auteur persona, the persona he cultivated with *Clerks*. The comparison of Smith's characters to Vladimir and Estragon was, in fact, made in 1994 by a New Jersey newspaper that described *Clerks* as "sort of a *Waiting for Godot* set in [New Jersey]" (Lumenick, E1). Holden reveals his artistic aspirations when discussing plans to produce a Bluntman and Chronic cartoon, remarking, "I don't know if that's really the perception I want people to have of our work. I know this sounds pretentious as hell, but I'd like to think of us as artists. And I'd like to get back to doing something more personal, like our first book." Holden is quite clearly expressing Smith's artistic side—the Smith that was praised by critics for apologizing for *Mallrats*.

Holden's partner Banky, in contrast, seems to represent the fanboy aspect of Smith's biography established in *Mallrats*. Accordingly, the character is portrayed by Jason Lee, the actor who had portrayed über-fanboy Brodie in the previous film. Banky seems to be Brodie transplanted from the realm of the comics fan to that of the comics professional. Even Banky's name is reminiscent of his predecessor.[13] He bristles when his artistic duty (that of inker) is mocked by someone as nothing but "tracing," the indignation calling to mind Brodie's anger over being referred to as a "sidekick." Banky becomes embroiled in a debate over the sexuality of Archie and Jughead reminiscent of Brodie's assertion that Lois Lane could not carry Superman's child. Like Brodie before him, Banky is Smith's main outlet for comic relief in *Chasing Amy*—until his goals and the more artistic goals of Holden come into conflict. Significantly, unlike Lee's Brodie, Lee's Banky is not the main character of *Chasing Amy*. Holden inarguably holds that position. Accordingly, the narrative presents Banky as subordinate to Holden in their creative ventures as well. While the pair co-write Bluntman & Chronic, Holden pencils the book, while Banky inks over his partner's pencils. Banky is thus presented as less of an artist than Holden. Banky's involvement with the film's main plot, that of the relationship between Holden and Alyssa, is largely tangential. He serves to introduce romantic tension between the two, but his presence in the film is secondary to that of Holden.

Keeping in mind both Holden's primacy to the story and the side of Smith he represents, consider Smith's comments regarding the character: "Holden is the closest to me I've ever written" (*Chasing Amy* DVD liner notes). Since Holden's relationship with Alyssa was modeled after Smith's relationship with Joey Adams (who plays Alyssa), it seems clear that Smith more forcefully aligns himself with Holden. In making him the focus of the film's narrative, Smith clearly aligns the viewer with Holden, as well. This connection is made before the conflict between Holden and Banky takes place.

The conflict ostensibly occurs because Banky feels that his relationship with Holden is threatened by the latter's romantic relationship. The conflict's primary manifestation, though, is the duo's disagreement over whether to go forth with the Bluntman and Chronic animated television series. After a particularly heated argument about Alyssa, Banky closes with the line, "You'd better be ready to make that deal!" Banky is concerned not only for his friendship with Holden, but also for the potential financial windfall from a highly commercial property that is being threatened by his partner's burgeoning 'seriousness'.

The deal, as it turns out, is not made. Banky and Holden go their separate ways after the climax of the film. A brief coda that takes place at a comic book convention brings the film full circle. Banky is shown at a booth for his new comic, *Baby Dave* (significantly, a Smith fan in-joke: Baby Dave is the on-set moniker of cinematographer Dave Klein). The same fan that opened the film by annoying Holden now asks Banky to sign a copy of the last issue of *Bluntman & Chronic*, titled "The Inevitable Death of Chronic."[14] When the fan asks Banky about "that other guy," Banky replies, "We don't talk." The fan praises Banky, saying "Look at how you draw a fart! Tell me you're not better off without him!" Banky, engaged in a wordless exchange with Holden, who stands across the room, distractedly replies, "You're so right." The fan smiles and says, "The true fans always are...love those dick jokes. Love 'em!"

Holden, on the other hand, is revealed to have returned to self-publishing with a comic titled *Chasing Amy*. The comic is based on his relationship with Alyssa, the relationship that formed the main plot of the film. When Alyssa sees the comic, she makes a comment that recalls an earlier scene in the movie and Smith's comments to the press regarding *Chasing Amy*:

Alyssa: Looks like a very personal story.
Holden: I finally had something personal to say.

Herein lies the resolution of the film's conflict. Holden has returned to a more personal art while the estranged Banky is relegated to garnering fanboy praise for the artistic quality of his rendering of flatulence. With which of these personas Smith aligns himself at the end of the film is hardly in question— Holden's comic is called *Chasing Amy*, after all. Thus does Smith present himself as having abandoned his Banky/*Mallrats*/fanboy persona in favor of the personal art of Holden/*Clerks*.

This agenda on the part of Smith within *Chasing Amy* is nowhere more apparent than in the one scene in the film in which Jay and Silent Bob appear. The scene, in which Holden delivers a royalty check to the duo, is rife with rejections of *Mallrats* and its fanboy aesthetic. Confronting Jay and Silent Bob about their tardiness, Holden mockingly asks, "What, were you at the mall again?" Jay curtly replies, "Bitch, don't even start. We stopped that shit years ago."

Not only is *Mallrats* rejected, the very conventions of Smith's continuity are broken. Silent Bob, instead of delivering one line near the film's climax (as he had in both *Clerks* and *Mallrats*), here launches into an entire monologue. Offering Holden counsel, he tells of a lost love and the lessons he took from it. The speech is utterly serious, and thus equates Smith (in his guise as Silent Bob) even further with Holden. It also subverts the expectations of the Smith fan. Silent Bob is, to the fan, the comic relief, the Jedi master from *Mallrats*. By injecting him into a dramatic situation, Smith-as-artist reclaims Silent Bob from Smith-as-fanboy. As Smith remarks in the film's liner notes, *Chasing Amy* serves Jay and Silent Bob by "returning to them the dignity they were stripped of when I swung them from the ceiling and had them chased by Keystonelike cops in *Mallrats*." Smith has instead chosen to have Silent Bob espouse the lesson of *Chasing Amy*—tell a personal story.

The rejection of *Mallrats* and its sensibilities comes once more in the scene, resulting from Jay asking Holden how many more royalty checks they have coming.

Holden: I don't know how much longer the comic's going to be around.
Jay: Yeah, good. I'll be glad as shit when it's gone.
Holden: There's a million people in the world who'd love to see themselves in a comic book.
Jay: But that ain't like us at all, all slapsticky and shit, running around like a couple of dickheads, saying…what's that shit he's got us saying?
Bob: Oh, uh…snoochie boochies.
Jay: Snoochie boochies. Who the fuck talks like that? That is

fucking baby talk!

The message seems clear—*Mallrats* and its brand of humor is in the past. Smith will no longer trade in "slapsticky" juvenile humor, choosing instead to focus on more personal stories. A positive critical response is unsurprising, given Smith's rejection of everything critics hated about *Mallrats* and his reintegration of the aspects of his biography they had loved, primarily the autobiographical storyteller element. The critics almost unanimously praised Smith for his newfound 'maturity' and 'honesty.' Some were even more upfront with their relief that Smith had rebounded from his sophomore effort. *Newsweek*'s David Ansen wrote, "Smith more than redeems himself [for *Mallrats*]: he grows up" (Ansen, 73). *Sight and Sound* commented, "*Chasing Amy* is [Smith's] first mature work" (Wrathall, 36). *The Los Angeles Times* described the film as "a work of ...fierce intelligence and emotional honesty" (Thomas, 12). Roger Ebert remarked that "this time, Silent Bob opens up with a heartfelt parable" (Ebert 1997, 35). In short, critics responded with the kind of praise that Holden (and, by extension, Smith's artist persona) would value.

Chasing Amy and its rejection of *Mallrats* had thus restored to Smith the mantle of 'artist' in the eyes of critics. But what of the fanboy persona that had germinated in the vacuum left in the wake of the critical abandonment of *Mallrats*? Having rejected it in a fairly overt way in *Chasing Amy*, was Smith consigning his fanboy side to purgatory?

The answer, unsurprisingly, is no. A total rejection of the fanboy persona and all of its trappings would likely have resulted in the fanboy's rejection of Smith in return. Rather than totally suppress his fanboy side, Smith divided the two personas, relegating each to a separate realm. Smith-as-artist continued as a filmmaker and a player in the independent film scene. Smith-as-fanboy, on the other hand, went underground, retreating to his origins—comics.

An Author Divided

In the wake of *Chasing Amy*, Smith's critical persona was largely defined by the promise at the end of that film—that of the artist who has chosen mature[15] personal expression over juvenile commercial fare. In the eyes of critics, Smith fulfilled this promise through the production and release of his fourth film, *Dogma*.

Described in the press materials as a "comedic fantasy," *Dogma* is the story of two fallen angels (Ben Affleck and Matt Damon) who attempt to reenter heaven through a loophole in Catholic doctrine. The heavenly host, upon learning of their plans, enlists abortion clinic employee Bethany (Linda Fiorentino) to stop the two. She is aided in her mission by Rufus (Chris Rock), the apocryphal thirteenth apostle (left out of the Bible because he was black) and two "prophets," Jay and Silent Bob. Amongst other things, the film asserts that Jesus was black, God is a woman and that Bethany is a direct descendant of the 'Virgin' Mary.

Unsurprisingly, the film met with protests and controversy. The anti-*Dogma* campaign was spearheaded by the Catholic League, an anti-defamation group unaffiliated with the Catholic Church proper. Primarily taking umbrage with the notion that Mary did not remain chaste after the Nativity, the Catholic League successfully lobbied Disney to force its subsidiary Miramax to dump the film (Jensen 1999, 37). Miramax heads Bob and Harvey Weinstein then purchased the film personally, a strategy they had earlier employed with the controversial film *Kids* (1995) (Carver, 1). The brothers, rather than release the film themselves, sold the distribution rights to Lions Gate Films, an up-and-coming art house outlet (Jones, 18). Lions Gate then released the film on November 12, 1999. This whole process was met with protest by religious groups. A letter-writing campaign aimed at Disney seems to have been responsible for Miramax's decision to sell the film. Nearly 1,500 protesters picketed the film's New York City premiere at the New York Film Festival (Rothman, F2). Both Smith and the Weinsteins claim to have received death threats in response to *Dogma*.

Throughout this prolonged process, Smith was quick to defend his film. "The movie's not an attack [on the church]," he told *Premiere*. "It's a challenge." He called the film "pro-faith," and asserted that, "If I had thought for a heartbeat that it was [blasphemous], I wouldn't have done it" ("Vanguard Dialogue...", 98). "Judging from the piles of hate mail," said Smith, "not every Catholic is a Christian" (LaSalle, 50).

Smith was quick to point out in every interview that he is a practicing Catholic, a fact that had rarely surfaced in interviews before and was never given the weight it acquired with *Dogma*. With *Dogma*, Smith's profession of faith before his interviewers becomes a mantra. The film, he claimed, came out of a crisis of faith he experienced in his early 20s. The idea came one Sunday during mass. "They call it the celebration of the Mass. It's not a party in there. Most people there are just terrified of going to hell. There's no enthusiasm for what's going on in there. And I thought, why? Aren't they jazzed about it? Don't they dig their own faith? So I wanted to make a movie about faith" (LaSalle, 50). Smith would later expound upon this in the DVD liner notes, writing,

While the seeds for *Dogma* were laid by eight years of Catholic school and a lifetime worth of Sunday masses, the passion to tell the story came solely from my unbridled appreciation for God...God's been good to me...Making a flick about the Lord was the least I could do...

Here we see Smith asserting that autobiographical elements formed the basis for *Dogma*, thus fulfilling the promise of *Chasing Amy*'s conclusion.

Critics responded in kind. While not as overwhelmingly positive in praise of *Dogma* as they had been of *Chasing Amy*, critics generally gave the film good reviews, often focusing on the personal nature of the story for Smith. In his three and a half star review, Roger Ebert wrote, "Kevin Smith's *Dogma* grows out of an irreverent modern Catholic sensibility." Ebert would go on to suggest that the film is so patently Catholic "that non-Catholics may need to be issued Catechisms on their way into the theater," highlighting the film's use of the obscure Catholic dogma of plenary indulgence as a major plot point (Ebert 1999, 33). "Because it tweaks conventional holy images, *Dogma* predictably has been attacked as blasphemous," said *The Boston Globe*. "But it's a film that only a sincere believer could make" (Carr, D1). Janet Maslin wrote, "With *Dogma* Mr. Smith makes a big, gutsy leap into questions of faith and religion. He miraculously emerges with his humor intact and his wings unsinged" (Maslin, E20). *Premiere* critic Glen Kenny called the film the most "theologically literate" film since Eric Rohmer's *My Night at Maud's* (1969) (Kenny, 86).

Critics also rallied to Smith's defense in regards to the controversy surrounding *Dogma*. Ebert, blasting the Catholic League, posited, "I think a Catholic God might plausibly enjoy a movie like *Dogma* (Ebert 1999, 33). Owen Gleiberman wrote, "I'm not sure that a movie has ever inspired a protest more fraught with irony than Kevin Smith's *Dogma*...Smith, make no mistake, is far from a blasphemer but, my God, does he love to tweak pieties!" (Gleiberman, 47). The assertion that the protesters were wrong to picket the film was mirrored by many critics. Smith was thus reaffirmed as an independent. By supposedly fighting conservative morals and being positioned as an auteur so dangerous that even Miramax could not touch him, Smith reemerged as a rebel outside the system. This battle and the role in which it cast Smith in the eyes of critics is reminiscent of the battle over the initial NC-17 rating slapped on *Clerks*. With *Dogma*, Smith is again the maverick, a position that primed critics to see him in a more favorable, artistic light (Levy, 52).

Dogma also led a leading film journal to reconsider the career of Smith. The November/December 1999 issue of *Film Comment*'s cover story used *Dogma* as a launching pad to revisit Smith's career-to-date. Author Robert Horton rehashes much of Smith's standard biography, but also rethinks the popular critical reception of *Mallrats*. After referring to it as "modest in its achievements," he goes on to write, "It's a lot of fun, though" (Horton, 63).

In another show of a return to his earliest biography, Smith was named as a Dramatic Competition Juror at the 2000 Sundance Film Festival. Smith parlayed the experience into a *Premiere* article, which he authored. In it, he creates his own awards as an excuse to relate anecdotes about the good, the bad and the ugly films he saw in Park City. "That way," he wrote, "we cover everybody—not just the really good flicks...but all the other crap I had to sit through as well" (Smith 2000, 50). Here, Smith has reclaimed a voice of authority in independent film that he had not presented publicly since *Spike, Mike, Slackers & Dykes*. The Kevin Smith of *Mallrats* could not have given a film "The 'Redford's Cousin Must've Made This Movie' Award,"[16] whereas the post-*Chasing Amy* and post-*Dogma* Smith can and does.

His reassumption of the 'voice of the filmmaker' mantle was also evidenced by his inclusion in the MTV documentary series "Nine for the 90s." The one-hour "Nine Movie Moments that Made the 90s" featured comments by many industry professionals and critics, but only two filmmakers, Smith and *Boyz 'n the Hood* (1991) helmer John Singleton (Torres, 21). Smith was featured in a segment highlighting the rise of the independent film, and is presented as the representative of the movement.

Not content simply to judge other's indie films, Smith

also began executive-producing independent films. Most of these films were made by his friends and View Askew cohorts, including *Vulgar* (2000), a film about a transvestite clown written and directed by Smith's friend Bryan Johnson (who plays comic shop owner Steve-Dave in Smith's films). Lion's Gate picked up the film for distribution at the 2000 Toronto Film Festival (Harris, 22). Smith has also produced a number of films that were not released theatrically, but that are available on DVD, including *A Better Place* (directed by Smith friend and View Askew historian Vincent Pereira), *Drawing Flies* (directed by Malcolm Ingram) and *Big Helium Dog* (directed by Brian Lynch). All of the films feature a cameo by Smith and star View Askew regulars like Brian O'Halloran and Jason Lee. Smith also executive produced Gus Van Sant's *Good Will Hunting* (1998). Smith was one of the first to read Affleck and Matt Damon's script and took it to Bob and Harvey Weinstein. The film went on to become Miramax's highest grossing to date (Brodie 1998, 83).

But what of Smith's fanboy persona? Seemingly abandoned at the end of *Chasing Amy*, the fanboy side of Smith's biography did not, in fact, disappear. Certainly, aspects of it can be seen in *Dogma*. Jay and Silent Bob return in their most prominent roles to date, and references are made to *Clerks*'s Quick Stop convenience store. At one point, Jay can be faintly heard offscreen relating one of the more 'slapsticky' episodes of *Mallrats* to another character. Continuity is preserved and furthered for the Smith fan, but perhaps more importantly, the offscreen line, probably only noticed by the dedicated (and repeat) viewer, defuses Jay's (and *Chasing Amy*'s) refutation of *Mallrats*. The average viewer (and critic) would likely never hear the line, though.

Dogma also serves to deepen Smith's continuity playground. The film establishes a good deal of information about everyday life in the View Askewniverse. Posters advertise Nails Cigarettes.[17] People eat at Mooby's, a fast food restaurant whose mascot is a ubiquitous Barney-like character. The leader in travel seems to be Derris, whose name is seen on trains and buses. By giving his world a depth beyond the narrative, Smith only encourages the entrenchment of the fan within said world. In addition, the creation of fake brand names allows for more merchandising opportunities. One can purchase a Zippo emblazoned with the Nails logo, or an official Mooby employee shirt.

While Kevin Smith fandom can find and enjoy the continuity references and expansions in *Dogma*, it is clear that the film does not revel in continuity to the degree that *Mallrats* and *Chasing Amy* did. It is perhaps unsurprising, then, that *Dogma* consistently ranks last when readers of the website *News Askew* are polled about their favorite Smith film. An Internet poll conducted in 2001 of over 5000 readers of *News Askew* found that only 13.4% ranked *Dogma* as their favorite Kevin Smith film, compared with *Mallrats* and *Chasing Amy*, which scored 24% and 28.5%, respectively.

A more complete expression of Smith's fanboy side found an outlet in the basement of pop culture—comic books. Award-winning comic author Warren Ellis wrote of comics: "...We're an outside art, a fringe medium watched by no-one but the more voracious cultural commentators and the aficionados" (Wood, introduction). In other words, the critical establishment would likely pay no attention to comics, leaving Smith free to express his fanboy persona to its fullest extent.

Smith's first foray into comics came in a roundabout way. After Miramax first screened *Chasing Amy* and realized that they had a critical hit on their hands, word of Smith's impending 'return' made the Hollywood rounds. Warner Brothers quickly contracted Smith to write two drafts of their planned return to the Superman franchise, based on the popular 'Death of Superman' comic book storyline (Brodie 1996, 1). Smith speculates that it was the discussion of Superman's sex life in *Mallrats* that landed him the job (*Mallrats* DVD). Whether true or not, Warner Brothers certainly saw in *Mallrats* and *Chasing Amy* that Smith understood the comic book audi-

The Dueling Personas of Kevin Smith

ence. Their instincts were correct, as the Internet comic community became enamored with Smith's draft of the script (which occasionally is posted online, and can also be purchased at comic book conventions), praising it for its faithfulness to the character.[18] The Superman draft opened other eyes as well. As *Wizard* magazine noted, "the comic book industry took notice of how seamlessly he blended the worlds of comics and film, prompting both Marvel and DC [the two principal comic companies, in terms of market share] to discuss hiring Smith to write some of their own high-profile characters" (Brick, 83).

Before trying his hand at others' comic characters, though, Smith attempted some of his own. His first comic writing, published in January of 1998, was the lead story in the anthology *Oni Double Feature* #1, titled "Jay & Silent Bob in: Walt Flanagan's Dog." The title is a reference to a throwaway line in *Mallrats*, in which Jay remarks that a security guard is "faster than Walt Flanagan's Dog." "Walt Flanagan's Dog" features characters from *Clerks* and *Mallrats* and is presented as taking place the night before the latter. In other words, it is dripping with continuity. In the story, Jay and Silent Bob get a dog stoned and are then chased by it—plotless hi-jinks reminiscent of the slapstick of *Mallrats*; the slapstick that Jay himself refuted in *Chasing Amy*. There is no personal story, a la Holden, to be found. Here, Jay and Silent Bob truly are more "Bill and Ted meet Cheech and Chong" than "Rosencrantz and Guildenstern meet Vladimir and Estragon."

The trend would continue in Smith's first full-length comic, published the next month, entitled simply *Clerks: The Comic Book*. In the comic, Dante and Randall become involved in the collectible *Star Wars* action figure business, uncovering the secret after-hours world of insider toy trading. Like "Walt Flanagan's Dog," this comic has nothing 'personal to say.' The *Clerks* of the title are stripped of any autobiographical angst that the film imbued them with, replacing it with slapstick and farfetched situations. And, of course, with *Star*

Wars references and debates. Smith would go on to publish two more *Clerks* comics, one a holiday special that ties up some of the film's loose ends (mainly the mental state of Dante's ex-girlfriend Caitlin) and a the other a comic version of an excised scene from the film. Again, neither seems to conform to the promise of the end of *Chasing Amy*, instead calling to mind the aesthetic of *Mallrats*. The audience for these comics is made even more clear in the *Wizard* magazine article announcing the *Clerks Holiday Special*: "All the little fanboys wishing for more *Clerks* comics can expect something better than coal in their stockings next month" (Hutchins, 27). Indeed, one of the main concerns of *Clerks: The Lost Scene* seems to be the regrounding of the film *Clerks* in View Askew continuity, as it introduces characters from later films into the narrative of the first View Askew film. In comic book terms, the retroactive addition of newer characters and situations to established 'history' is known as 'retconning,' and this certainly seems to be what Smith is attempting.

Smith also turned to the major comic book publishers, taking on scripting duties for eight issues on Marvel's *Daredevil* in 1998. The series made Smith a superstar in the comics industry. He sat atop the *Wizard* "Top 10 Writers" list for most of 1999. In February of 1999, Smith's *Daredevil* #1 sat in the top position of *Wizard*'s "Top 10 Comics" while *Jay & Silent Bob* #1 held the second position. The December 1998 "Top 10 Comics" even referred to the "obligatory Kevin Smith part of our countdown."

Smith also published an eponymously titled four-part limited series featuring Jay and Silent Bob, later collected under the title *Chasing Dogma*. The series served to detail the duo's travels from the New Jersey diner in *Chasing Amy* to the Illinois abortion clinic in *Dogma*, filling in the continuity gaps. While the prior scene is a very dramatic personal one (in which Silent Bob delivers his monologue) and the latter leads to some personal ruminations upon faith and God, the adventures that come in between are anything but personal. Jay and Bob wander onto a porno set, help an escaped monkey and battle government agents in Smith's most *Mallrats*-like comic to date. The episode with the monkey, in fact, tells the story of Suzanne, the orangutan shown at the end of *Mallrats*. The series at one point calls to mind the fan's response to Banky's comic at the end of *Chasing Amy*—Jay is drawn farting on Silent Bob.

The next comic to feature Smith's own characters makes it completely clear that the resolution of *Chasing Amy* was not as final as it seemed. *Oni Double Feature* #12 featured a Bluntman and Chronic story. The return of the *Mallrats* analogue drives home the idea that Smith's resolution to tell personal stories applies only to films. In fact, Smith has plans to produce a sequel to *Mallrats* in comic form, titled *Mallrats 2: Die Hard in a Mall* (*Mallrats* DVD, Director's Commentary). Apparently, the "inevitable death of Chronic" and of Smith-as-fanboy was not as permanent as it seemed.[19] In comics, a medium that can go largely unseen by critics, Smith is free to exercise his inner Banky. As Smith commented in a *Wizard* interview, "I've lived the ultimate fanboy's life. To cross between both worlds and work in the medium that you love [film], then to be working in a new medium that you love too, love even *more* to some degree, it's pretty damn thrilling" (Brick, 83).

Smith would also break new ground in a third medium: the Internet. Smith emerged as a filmmaker at roughly the same time that the Internet was beginning to emerge as a powerful cultural force (due largely to the introduction of graphical browsers like Netscape), and his early embrace of the technology put him at the forefront of the film industry's slow realization of the web as a marketing tool. Smith's early forays into Internet content, however, were grounded largely in the traditions and forms of a medium he was already well-versed in: comic books.

Pustz notes that the Internet is a natural extension of the comic book culture. Especially in its early days, the web was a haven for a culture whose stereotype has much in common with the notion of the fanboy (recall that *The Simpsons'* Comic Book Guy is also represented as an Internet geek). Jenkins, writing in 1992, examined the earliest expressions of this movement to the electronic within the fan culture, focusing on the use of newsgroups in the cultivation and maintenance of *Twin Peaks* fandom (Jenkins 1995, 78).

Furthermore, the Internet is able to perform the functions of the letters page often found in comic books and of the independently published 'fanzine' (Pustz, 188). Both kinds of fan interaction are crucial to the development and maintenance of comic book culture. Both were also appropriated by Smith when he introduced *www.viewaskew.com*.

The fan-produced website is an electronic version of what the fanzine had been. Produced and distributed by fans, the fanzine is a prime example of 'textual poaching,' as defined by Jenkins. According to Pustz, the fanzine served as an outlet for fans to share a love of a certain character or creator through trivia, games and original stories and art. Through such an interaction with texts, fans are drawn closer to the texts and the sense of identification with the text is reinforced (Jenkins 1992, 45). Fan-produced websites perform many of the same functions and have proliferated in the 1990s (Pustz, 181-4).

Fansites devoted to Kevin Smith began to surface in 1995. Smith, upon connecting to the Internet for the first time that year, was particularly impressed by a website devoted to *Clerks*. Smith contacted the site's designer, Ming-Si Chen, and hired him to design an official site. In March of 1996, *www.viewaskew.com* went live. Aside from the fairly standard 'official' website content (profiles of Smith and his filmmaking cohorts, character biographies for both *Clerks* and *Mallrats*, etc.), Viewaskew.com features a message board in which fans could interact with each other as well as with Smith. This message board functions in much the same way as the letter column in comics which exist at the boundary between fans and creators, readers and content...[the interaction] may occur in isolation from the rest of the media world, but it only helps to intensify the boundaries created in the process. Fans gain an identity and have it strengthened through awareness of others involved in similar activities. This awareness—and the feeling of fellowship it creates—begins in the letter pages (Pustz, 177).

The letter column has largely been phased out of mainstream comics, primarily due to the immediacy of the Internet as a feedback tool. Brooker, writing on Internet fandom, shows that a similar effect to that of the lettercol can be achieved online, writing, "Internet boards...allow any reader to instantly become a participating writer on an equal footing with fellow contributors, including the site's creator or even the published authors who occasionally visit to post their own responses to discussion" (Brooker, 55). Smith became more than an occasional visitor to *viewaskew.com*; he frequently posted answers to questions, opinions of other people's films and comics and good-natured barbs at other board posters.[20]

Interacting with fans in this way allows Smith to solidify his fan base, much like comic book letter columns did in the past. The importance of this to the establishment of both his fanboy persona and the audience it cultivated cannot be overlooked. Recall that, in addition to the traditional concept of defining a fan by his or her actions (like the extra-narrative engagement of a text), a fan is also defined by a sense of subcultural identity. It was through the Internet that fans engaging with Smith's material could find a sense of community among others who did the same, thus creating and reaffirming an identity as a 'Kevin Smith fan.' Pustz does not overstate his case when he notes that "without lettercols [and, as we have seen, Internet boards], comic book culture might not exist at all" (Pustz, 177). The same may be true of Smith's fanboy audience and, by extension, his fanboy persona.

Smith's fanboy persona was also bolstered by his embrace

of another technology—DVD. DVD, though in its infancy thought of as fundamentally a cinephile's format, holds enormous appeal within the realm of fandom. The ability of the technology to present fans with copious amounts of ancillary material and 'behind the scenes' information in a user-friendly format and an affordable package has been well-utilized by Smith. Each View Askew DVD also features an audio commentary track in which Smith, producer Scott Mosier and assorted cast and crew members discuss the film. Rather than providing much insight into the production and or themes of the movies, though, the commentaries tend to seem more akin to a reunion party. To wit, on the *Clerks* commentary, recorded in a hotel room during the production of *Mallrats*, a drunken Jason Mewes passes out, audibly snoring at one point. The assembled guests often spend time good-naturedly mocking Ben Affleck, poking fun at actors they did not like and taking half-hearted potshots at Smith's lack of cinematic aplomb. Throughout, Smith comes across as affable and laid-back. This access to and seeming immediacy of the filmmaker reinforces the fanbase in much the same way that his interaction with fans on the Internet does.

With Smith's entry into the comic book industry proper and the trade press' subsequent coverage of his work, added to the regular interaction with fans that took place on his website, the fanboy persona began to acquire the details and background necessary to become a full-fledged biography. Facts about his tastes in comics, his opinions of past creators and characters and his ambitions in the industry serve to flesh out his persona. For example, one of the details of his fanboy biography concerned his marriage to journalist Jennifer Schwalbach. Though his marriage is a subject that often comes up in mainstream outlets (Smith's Sundance piece in *Premiere*, for example), a significant detail of the wedding was reported only in the comic book press (and on Smith's website). The two were married at George Lucas' Skywalker Ranch in April 1999 during postproduction on *Dogma* (McLauchlin 1999, 70). The parallels to T.S.' wedding at the end of *Mallrats* on the Jaws ride at the Universal Studios tour is uncanny. One can hardly imagine a more fanboyish place to get married, given the fanboy tendency to approach Lucas with a sort of "deification" (Brooker, 68). In addition, the couple named their first daughter, Harley Quinn Smith, after a character created for the Batman animated series. One need not wonder which of the parents suggested that name.

One of the more interesting and relevant details that comes to light is Smith's purchase of a Red Bank, NJ comic book store in late 1997. When the previous owner moved away, he presented Smith with the opportunity to buy the store. "I'd always planned one day, maybe when I was burned out and had no more stories to tell, I'd just kick back and run a comic book store. So I bought it, revamped it, and turned it into [Jay and Silent Bob's] Secret Stash" (Brick, 86). Relating his involvement with the business to *Wizard*, he creates connections to his *Clerks* days. "I'm pretty much there at least once or twice a day. Sometimes I'll just sit there and spend the whole day; sometimes it's just nice to sit and work the register, doing that register jockey thing" (Brick, 86). Smith moved the Secret Stash into a new location in early 1999 and held a fan festival to celebrate the occasion. Dubbed the 'Stash Bash,' the festival was attended by over 400 fans, featured tours of *Clerks* filming locations, autograph sessions and film screenings at night. The Secret Stash now sells such fanboy ephemera as T-shirts, posters and autographed DVDs and comics. It is referred to on the View Askew message boards as 'Mecca for Kevin Smith fans,' and a visit makes that statement easy to believe. While the shelves and racks are filled with a myriad of Kevin Smith products for sale, the walls are adorned with props, costumes and production art from all of Smith's movies (Figure 7). Essentially, Jay and Silent Bob's Secret Stash is as much a museum as it is a comic shop.

Figure 7: A museum-like display within Jay and Silent Bob's Secret Stash

In a *Wizard* article, the interviewer remarked, "You're living the ultimate fanboy's fantasy—you make movies, write comics and own your own comic shop." Reflecting on this, Smith replied, "Geez, what's left right? Yes, there is one more thing left before it's all complete, and that's action figures. As soon as they do the Jay and Silent Bob action figures, then I know I'm fulfilled, I've lived the ultimate fanboy's life" (Brick, 86). The Stash began selling Jay and Silent Bob action figures in mid-1999, followed by Bluntman and Chronic action figures were released in the Summer of 2002.

Following a well-traveled path from toys to cartoons, Smith further proved that his fanboy persona was not bound to the conclusion of *Chasing Amy* by developing an animated series based on *Clerks*. Whereas *Chasing Amy* presented Holden as reluctant to allow his creations to be turned into cartoons (recall his line, "I'm not sure if that's the impression I want people to have of our work."), Smith was eager to push his creation into an animated outlet. "No matter what happens," he told *Wizard*, "even if it tanks, I say we made it already. It's every boy's dream, ain't it? A cartoon of their own" (McLauchlin 1999, 70).

The show did, in fact, 'tank,' and only two episodes of the cartoon aired on ABC in May of 2000. The show was intended as pure comedy, with none of the more serious elements that elicited some of the higher praise of the film version of *Clerks*. The cartoon seems to be very much aimed at the Kevin Smith fanboy, as it is rife with subtle nods to continuity and to comic book sensibilities. The last five minutes of the first aired episode ends in a five minute *anime* parody—hardly the sort of humor that wins over a mainstream primetime audience. Perhaps this accounts for the show's short and relatively quiet lifespan. Smith did not abandon the show, however. The VHS and DVD versions of the series were be released in early 2001 and included the four episodes that were produced but not aired. The DVD release of the series, titled *Clerks: Uncensored* features commentary tracks on each of the six episodes, as well as production designs and animatics, in keeping with the precedent set by the DVDs of Smith's films.

The final episode of the series, appropriately titled "The Last Episode Ever," contains a scene that is puzzling, given that the series seems so geared towards fandom. The episode begins as the frame pans past a number of people dressed in superhero costumes, one of whom is picking his nose, finally coming to rest on the sign outside of the convention hall, pictured here:

The scene cuts to inside, and shows Dante and Randall walking past a number of booths, the signs above which advertise "The Guy Who Cleaned Out Latrines on the Episode I Shoot" and "The Woman Who Did Captain Kirk." Essentially, this sequence mocks fan interests and activities, especially the extremes to which they will go to get close to the producers of media.

Dante: Ready to meet our adoring fans?
Randall: After you.

Figure 8: A jab at fandom from Clerks: The Cartoon

The pair enter a room only to find four convention goers and a homeless man sleeping in the front row. After expressing some bewilderment, the pair sit down in the front of the room.

Dante: Uh, hi loyal fans. I'm Dante and this is Randall. We're the stars of the hit ABC cartoon *Clerks* and we're here to take your questions…
Fan #1: Yeah, I loved the movie *Clerks*, but I think your show sucks hard. It's in color and nobody curses. It's nothing like the movie…
Randall: That wasn't even a question.
Fan #2: Yeah, I wanted to ask how little you guys sold out for, and what it feels like to have no soul and a black heart?
Dante: I can't believe it. They hate the show.

While it could be argued that Smith is reveling in a bit of self-mockery (much like Brodie using the term 'fanboy' derogatively in *Mallrats*), his comments on the DVD commentary seem to preclude that possibility. Smith reveals that that scene was included specifically to preempt criticisms from fans who may have felt that the cartoon strayed too far from its filmic roots. This amounts to a disavowal, or, worse, a dismissal of the sort of obsessive engagement of texts and intertextual comparisons that fandoms often revel in. Smith seems to be venting some hostility towards fandom in a way that seems antithetical to his attitude since the resolution of *Chasing Amy*. In fact, this seems like one of the jokes that are made at the expense of the fan who harasses Holden at the comic book convention. Smith's ambiguous attitude toward fandom would return in what would, on the surface, seem to be an unlikely place—Smith's fifth film and self-avowed "love letter to the fans," *Jay and Silent Bob Strike Back*.

Before examining that film, though, it should be noted that, prior to its release, most critics seem to have taken no notice of Smith's fan base since its creation and growth.[21] His critical reputation seems to have almost fully diverged from his reputation as a fan-favorite director. Banky and Holden truly "don't talk." This stands in contrast to other cinematic figures whose cultish fan base becomes a defining part of their biographies. John Waters and other 'midnight movie' auteurs are examples of this latter type. As the example from *Clerks: Uncensored* suggests, though, the divide between Smith's fanboy and critical personae would soon narrow.

Blurring the Line

Kevin Smith, having seemingly disavowed his fanboyish tendencies at the resolution of *Chasing Amy*, had kept himself in the good graces of critics by readopting many of the facets of his *Clerks*-era critical biography. At the same time, Smith was catering to his fanbase by creating comics and interacting with them on his website, solidifying a separate fanboy biography. These personas remained largely separate, with critics seemingly unaware of the fanboy aspects of Kevin Smith's biography. In the period leading up to the release of his next film, *Jay and Silent Bob Strike Back*, however, the borders dividing the two personas began to break down.

Smith's plans for his fifth film were first revealed as a tagline at the end of *Dogma*, which touted, "Jay and Silent Bob will return in *Clerks 2: Hardly Clerkin'*." Smith claimed that he wanted to make one final film in his "View Askew Chronicles," and thought that it would be appropriate to bookend the series by returning to the milieu that had started his film career (View Askew message board). Though the planned sequel to Smith's first film was quickly abandoned, the idea behind it lingered. Smith wanted to make the final film a "love letter" to his fans, and, as such, would adopt the style of the one that had solidified his fanbase—*Mallrats*.

We're going to do…a real balls to the wall comedy, kind of like 'Rats, which tanked. But we're trying to do a little history correcting here, and make a flat-out comedy that succeeds this time. Plus, the last two were funny but also weighty, and it just feels like it's time to do one that's nothing but funny, with no message or anything, especially after what happened to us on the last one, with all the hate mail and death threats (Smith, *Psycomic* website).

Figure 9: Logo as homage

Smith fans responded positively to this return to form, as evidenced by the results of a poll on *NewsAskew*, which asked the following intriguingly worded question: "Were you happy to hear that Kevin is going back to the roots (*and away from personal stories*) for the next film [emphasis added]?" Two-thirds of the over 1000 respondents replied in the affirmative, with only 17% voting 'no'.[22]

In keeping with this fan-friendly attitude for his fifth feature, Smith aggressively marketed the film online. The film's title was first revealed online, and, unsurprisingly, the title itself was a nod to fandom. *Jay and Silent Bob Strike Back*, proclaimed a logo strikingly reminiscent of *The Empire Strikes Back* (20th Century Fox, 1981) (Figure 9).

Smith continued to provide his fans with a high level of access to the filmmaking process using the Internet. Through an online column, named "Developing the Monkey," on the now-defunct site *Psycomic*, Smith related stories of casting the film, detailing 'meet-and-greets' with David Duchovny, Shannon Elizabeth and Judd Nelson, among others. He also maintained an on-set diary on the View Askew website, and regularly checked in with fans on the message boards during the shoot. Smith also held a contest online in which readers could send in pictures of themselves, possibly to be used in a shot in the film. The film was also promoted online by *Ain't-It-Cool-News*, who sent their contributor 'Mysterio' to the set of *Jay and Silent Bob Strike Back*. 'Mysterio's' experiences were related in a series of long articles on *AICN*, adding to the film's visibility among members of fandom.

Taking a cue from the successful Internet marketing campaigns of *The Blair Witch Project* (Artisan, 1999) and *A.I.* (Dreamworks, 2001), Smith also generated a fair amount of buzz by creating a fictitious website to promote the film. On May 10, 2001, Smith posted to his message board, writing, "...I'm going to finally... FINALLY... give some motherfuckers in cyberworld the bitch-slapping they've been begging for for months. I'm in a bridge-burning mood, folks. Grab your marshmallows." Smith had become notorious within the online comics community for his feuds with other comic creators and his merciless panning of others' movies. As a result, Smith's post was taken quite seriously, and the news popped up on many comics and film-related news sites. Smith came online later that night and posted a link to a new movie website, one which was "mouthing off" about his films. Encouraging people to carefully read the site, Smith directed them to *Movie Poop Shoot* at www.moviepoopshoot.com. There, fans found a carefully-constructed parody of *Ain't-It-Cool-News*, and when a visitor clicked on the hyperlink that would lead to a story panning *Jay and Silent Bob Strike Back*, the reader was treated to an Internet-exclusive trailer of the film. *Movie Poop Shoot*, as Smith soon revealed, was a fictional website created by him and webmaster Ming Chen, and would play a major role in *Jay and Silent Bob Strike Back*.

Smith went on to create another fake website to promote the film, and this time the stunt caught the attention of the mainstream press. Smith created a site titled, "The Official Strike Back Against *Jay and Silent Bob Strike Back*." Located at www.jayandsilentbobstrikeback.com, the site had all of the hallmarks of a 'squatter' site—a site that reserves the domain name of a legitimate film in order to bash that film. *USA Today* picked up on the chicanery, and Smith revealed that he had created the site to promote the film. "He decided on a whim to put up the site as an extension of the film's plot, which involves Internet name-calling," the paper reported (Kornblum "Director...", 3D). In this way it recalls the masterful online promotion of Spielberg's *A.I.* (Kornblum "*A.I.* ...", E1) . Smith used the Internet to involve fans in a sort of game, sending them on a scavenger hunt across the web. Obviously, such a device can only serve to more fully involve fans in the narrative of the texts.

The film was also heavily promoted in the comics industry press, garnering especially extensive coverage from *Wizard*, who published reports from the set and ran a contest in which a reader could win a walk-on part (McLauchlin 2001, 30-3). The *Wizard* coverage culminated in a special issue devoted entirely to Kevin Smith. The director, in full Bluntman regalia, also graced the cover of *Previews*, the monthly catalog of upcoming comic projects.

The comics industry was squarely behind Smith, and, given the film's plot, this is unsurprising. *Jay and Silent Bob*

Strike Back details the titular duo's discovery that Miramax is producing a film version of *Bluntman & Chronic*, the comic created by the protagonists of *Chasing Amy*. The pair, realizing that they have yet to be compensated for the use of their likenesses, track down Holden McNeil, who informs them that the Internet buzz surrounding the film is intense. Venturing online, Jay and Silent Bob find the website *Movie Poop Shoot*, on which they find "net nerds" anonymously slandering them and their fictional alter-egos, Bluntman and Chronic. Determined to preserve their "good names," the two vow to put a stop to this, and decide that the only way to do so is to stop the movie from being made. Jay and Bob light out from New Jersey for Hollywood.

The film then adopts a road movie structure, in which the pair have a series of cameo-heavy episodic adventures on the way to Hollywood, including encounters with an unnamed gang of teenagers reminiscent of the gang from *Scooby-Doo*, a group of *Charlie's Angels*-esque jewel thieves and an escaped orangutan named Suzanne. In the course of the film, the two are mistaken for international terrorists and are pursued by the authorities.

When Jay and Silent Bob finally arrive in Hollywood, the film parodies a number of films, including the Smith-produced *Good Will Hunting* and the *Scream* franchise. The duo finally find the *Bluntman and Chronic Strike Back* set, but, unable to stop production, settle for one-half of executive producer Banky Edwards' share of the profits. The pair use that money to fly around the country and assault all of the people who slandered them on the Internet. The film culminates at the premiere of the *Bluntman & Chronic* film, which finds characters from all four of Smith's previous films in attendance.

That this movie would appeal to Kevin Smith's fans is no surprise. It is easily the most thoroughly grounded in continuity of all of his films. In fact, the film follows Jay and Silent Bob through the Askewniverse, visiting characters in the order in which the films were made. *Jay and Silent Bob Strike Back* opens outside of *Clerks'* Quick Stop, and Dante and Randall make a cameo. Jay and Bob then visit *Mallrats'* Brodie at the comic shop he owns, followed by a visit to *Chasing Amy*'s Holden. The *Dogma* references are more subtle, perhaps reflecting that film's relative lack of popularity with Smith fans. The references do exist though, as just after the duo leave Holden's loft, they encounter both *Dogma* co-star George Carlin and a nun who has *Dogma*'s 'Buddy Christ' as a dashboard statue. Throughout the course of the film, the pair also encounter Walt and Steve-Dave, the comic shop employees from *Mallrats*, Hooper X, Banky and Alyssa from *Chasing Amy*, and Alyssa's sister Trisha, who was a character in *Mallrats*. The film closes with Alanis Morrissette as *Dogma*'s God literally closing the book on 'The View Askewniverse.'

The film gives another nod to the comic book audience by presenting the viewer with Jay and Silent Bob's 'origin.' The revelation of the origins of comic book characters is always a major event, and often the issue in which the origin is revealed becomes highly collectible. The opening scenes of the movie detail how the pair were left in front of the Quick Stop as infants, and are implicated through time-lapse dissolve to have been hanging out there ever since (Figure 10). The roots of Jay's profanity are seen in the character of his mother.

The film is also rife with references to Smith's real life and his interaction with the fan community. One of the Internet posters on the *Movie Poop Shoot* website that so enrages Jay and Bob is named 'Magnolia Fan,' referencing Smith's diatribe against Paul Thomas Anderson's *Magnolia* (New Line, 1999); a rant that *Entertainment Weekly* called "legendary" ("It Dirt Disher", 105). Moreover, Magnolia Fan is the name of a real-life reader/contributor on *Ain't-It-Cool-News*, and who is known for his anti-Kevin Smith diatribes.

Figure 10: The origin of Jay and Silent Bob

Brodie, who was earlier shown to be the idealized fanboy and the character most representative of Smith's fanboy persona, has an interesting cameo in the film. The über-fanboy is shown to run a comic book shop named Brodie's Secret Stash in downtown Red Bank, New Jersey. A knowledgeable fan would notice that the storefront in question is actually Smith's comic shop, Jay and Silent Bob's Secret Stash (Figure 11). Smith is reasserting his kinship with Brodie in the eyes of the fan.

Jay and Silent Bob Strike Back also pokes fun at itself, primarily through the character of Holden. When Jay and Bob ask about their cut of the profits from the *Bluntman & Chronic* movie, Holden replies,

Holden: I got nothing to do with it. That's Banky's deal. He owns the property now. I sold my half of the *Bluntman & Chronic* rights to him years ago.
Jay: Why the fuck would you do a thing like that?
Holden: Why in God's name would I want to keep writing about characters whose central preoccupation is weed and dick and fart jokes? I mean, you gotta grow, man. Don't you ever want anything more for yourself? (Points at Silent Bob) I know this poor, hapless son of a bitch does. I look

into his sorry doe eyes and I just...I see a man crying out, 'When Lord? When the fuck can your servant ditch this foul-mouthed little chucklehead to whom I am a constant victim of his folly...?

Figure 11: The Secret Stash in fiction and reality

As Holden's speech draws to a close, Silent Bob nods in stunned agreement, then looks at Jay, and shakes his head dismissively.

By using Holden, a character Smith had previously associated with personal storytelling and artistic integrity, to dismiss the film the audience is watching, Smith is obviously mocking his own misgivings about making another *Mallrats-*

style comedy. Given the film's previous association of Smith with Brodie only moments prior, this scene might seem counter-productive to the film's fan-friendly stance. Rather than seriously engaging the topic of artistic integrity, though, Holden's artistic disavowal of the goings-on in *Jay and Silent Bob Strike Back* are played for laughs. This is made patently apparent when, asked about the *Bluntman & Chronic* movie, he notes, "I don't think I'm alone in imagining this flick might be the worst idea since Greedo shooting first[23]...you know, a Jay and Silent Bob movie—who'd pay to see that?" At this point, everyone turns and looks at the camera, and Silent Bob sheepishly smiles.

The film fulfills Smith's promise as a return to *Mallrats*-like comedy, going so far as to recreate Silent Bob's use of the *Batman*-esque grappling hook from the 1995 film. The *Mallrats* connection is reinforced even further when one considers that the entire film is based around *Bluntman & Chronic*, which served as an analogue for *Mallrats* within the narrative of *Chasing Amy*.

Unlike *Mallrats*, however, *Jay and Silent Bob Strike Back* was not unanimously panned by critics. In fact, early test screenings prompted the following post from Smith on his website, dated July 4, 2001:When I was writing this flick, I felt I might be sacrificing the critical reaction for the fan reaction. I thought it was a fair trade-off to make, as I was more concerned with putting together a flick you guys would get off on than making a film the critics jizzed over (although with a three out of four record - 'Clerks', 'Amy' and 'Dogma' - I won't lie; it was a tough decision; when it comes to critical jizz, I'm into the facials; toss me them pearl necklaces, I say). I guess I'd assumed a while ago that critics and the press weren't going to dig on this movie like they dug on three of our four others flicks, because this flick was closer in tone to the one they DIDN'T like (poor l'il 'Rats).

The shocker is that with the exception of maybe three single hold-outs, all 200 plus of the print/radio/and TV media folks at the junket dug the flick. And I mean DUG it. Same was true out of the NY press screenings - the press really loved the movie.

I'm flabbergasted.

In the final analysis, reviewers were not quite as enamored with the film as Smith had anticipated (or as they had led him to believe after its press screening), and published reviews were fairly evenly divided between the positive and the negative. Still, this is a far cry from the critical disappointment in and dismissal of Smith that *Mallrats* prompted. The difference can be attributed to a few factors.

First, it must be acknowledged that, cinematically, *Jay and Silent Bob Strike Back* is light years beyond *Mallrats*, and, indeed, the rest of Smith's oeuvre. Unlike any of Smith's previous four films, *Jay and Silent Bob Strike Back* looks like a Hollywood film. The movie is glossy and uses color well, and the camerawork is fluid for the first time in a Smith film. Most of the critics fail to mention this in their reviews, but, for that matter, most do not criticize his visuals, either.

Narratively, the film also moves much more quickly than *Mallrats* did, and the adoption of the road movie genre seems to have pleased many critics. *Premiere*'s Glenn Kenny pointed out the film's similarity to the classic Hope/Crosby road movies (Kenny, 86). *USA Today* agreed, noting, "It's the first movie in a half-century to recapture the spirit of '40s comedies in which a few dozen stars appeared to parody their images" (Clark, E1).

Critics were also likely swayed by the links in the film to some of the already-established facets of Smith's critical persona. The film, while quite farcical, obviously grows out of Smith's own Hollywood experiences, making *Jay and Silent Bob Strike Back*, in some ways, a personal story.[24] Much of the humor in the film, aside from being inside jokes for Smith fans, consists of inside jokes for those in and around the film business. Many references are made in the film to Miramax, with whom Smith had developed a very public business relationship, and many jokes are had at the Weinstein's expense.

Jay: Miramax? I thought they only made classy pictures like *The Piano* or *The Crying Game*.
Brodie: Yeah, well, once they made *She's All That*, everything went to hell.

Critics may have also been more likely to embrace *Jay and Silent Bob Strike Back* knowing that it was to be the last of Smith's 'Askewniverse' films, a fact that many bring up in reviews. This could be especially true in light of Smith's public plans for his next film, a film about fatherhood based on his own experiences. Interestingly, a few critics seemed to lament the fact that Smith was retiring the Jay and Silent Bob characters. Glenn Kenny closed his review by wishing that Smith would do more comedies with the pair (Kenny, 86). This is a far cry from Kenneth Turan's post-*Mallrats* statement that the return of Jay and Silent Bob "feels…like a threat."

Critics also were able to rally around Smith in the face of controversy, much as they had previously done in the cases of *Clerks'* NC-17 rating and *Dogma*'s religious protests. Despite Smith's earlier claim to want to make a film "that's nothing but funny, with no message or anything, especially after what happened to us on the last one," *Jay and Silent Bob Strike Back* was met with protests from GLAAD, the Gay and Lesbian Alliance Against Defamation, who took offense at the film's many jokes about homosexuality. Critics rushed to Smith's defense in their reviews. Roger Ebert noted that GLAAD had picked "the wrong" target in attacking the film, adding, "GLAAD should give audiences credit for enough intelligence to know the difference between satire and bigotry" (Ebert 2001, 31). Other critics agreed, for while some showed disdain for the film's over-the-top vulgarity, no mainstream critics sided with GLAAD. Smith, for his part, donated $10,000 to the Matthew

Shepard Foundation and added a disclaimer to the end credits denouncing hate speech (Jensen 2001, 104).

However, the most surprising facet of both the positive and negative reviews is the near-unanimous acknowledgement of several aspects of Smith's fanboy persona. *The Houston Chronicle* calls Smith "our comic-book-reading, *Star Wars*-geeking, pot-and-sex-joking perpetual adolescent," who "has not abandoned his geek past but embraced it" (Moore, 10). The article goes on to mention Smith's comic book writing and the existence of the Jay and Silent Bob action figures. Roger Ebert began his review by noting, "It is becoming clear that the film universe of Kevin Smith is interconnected, that characters from one movie can expect to run into characters from another—like Faulkner's Yoknapatawpha County, Smithland has a permanent population, even though we may not meet all of them in every movie[25]" (Ebert 2001, 31). Another critic noted that "*Jay and Silent Bob Strike Back* represents the ultimate wish-fulfillment for filmmaker Kevin Smith, the professional fanboy now idolized by thousands if not millions of similarly comic book-craving, *Star Wars*-addicted, TV rerun-saturated, Internet-surfing…American males" (Beifuss, E1). Even the negative reviews recognize the fanboy persona, as this lengthy-yet-informative quote from the *Houston Press* shows:

Beware the filmmaker who looks through the camera's lens and sees only himself on the other side, blowing kisses…Kevin Smith is one such filmmaker, and for the fetishists and fanboys who obsess over his DVDs, loaded with hours of outtakes and commentary, that's not really a problem. They immerse themselves in his so-called Askewniverse…and dare not pester the creator, no matter how decrepit the surroundings have become. They groove on the inside jokes—which is all Kevin Smith movies have become, especially now…Smith long ago stopped being a filmmaker and instead turned into a franchise-maker…Smith the filmmaker has become Smith the comic-book writer, meaning he's obsessed with such things as continuity and cosmology at the expense of coherence and accessibility (Wilonsky, 50).

Ebert puts a more egalitarian spin on that reviewer's closing arguments, writing, "Whether you will like *Jay and Silent Bob* depends on who you are. Most movies are made for everybody. Kevin Smith's movies are either made specifically for you, or specifically not made for you" (Ebert 2001, 31). Based on his review, Ebert clearly places himself in the former category.

As the boundaries between the fanboy and critical personas clearly have become more permeable, where does this leave Kevin Smith fandom? As has already been noted, part of the appeal of fandom is the outsider, underground status of the subject matter. Once critics are privy to the workings of the fanboy persona, even, in some cases, praising the fanboyish nature of the film, the subcultural appeal is in danger of dissipating. Smith, rather than taking overt steps to maintain his subcultural fanboy appeal, seems to instead act in ways to undermine it. Expanding upon the dismissal and ridicule of fan culture already noted in *Clerks: The Cartoon*, this is best exemplified in *Jay and Silent Bob Strike Back* by a scene in which Smith topples one of the main pillars upon which his fandom rests—continuity.

The astute reader may have noticed that one scene described in bed in *Jay and Silent Bob Strike Back* seems reminiscent of an earlier description of a Smith story. In the film, Jay and Silent Bob liberate an orangutan named Suzanne from an animal testing lab. Pursued by a federal wildlife marshal in a setup reminiscent of *The Fugitive*, the pair has a series of misadventures with the ape. In one scene, Jay theorizes that Suzanne is a 'super chimp,' and the film launches into an elaborate *Planet of the Apes* parody. Later, Jay, Silent Bob and Suzanne are cornered by the authorities, escaping only by pretending to be a homosexual couple traveling with their adopted child.

This whole episode is meant to fill in the question raised in the coda of *Mallrats*—in which Jay and Silent Bob were shown walking down a highway with an orangutan between them, while a caption noted, "Suzanne? Jay and Silent Bob? That's a whole different story." To the average viewer, then, this would seem to simply tell the story promised in the earlier film. To the dedicated Kevin Smith fan, however, this story has already been told. As noted earlier, Suzanne was the centerpiece of the third issue of the comic book *Chasing Dogma*. Indeed, most of the comic is imported word-for-word into *Jay and Silent Bob Strike Back*.

This would seemingly carry major implications for the Kevin Smith fan. After all, the *Jay and Silent Bob* comic series was intended to explain how the duo went from the diner in *Chasing Amy* to the abortion clinic in *Dogma*. By lifting a major scene from the comic and transplanting it into *Jay and Silent Bob Strike Back*, Smith is essentially negating that bit of continuity. Breaches in continuity have always been scorned by comics fandom. Until recently, Marvel Comics would award a prize to any reader that could prove that the company had violated the coherence of its universe. That Smith, admittedly vested in continuity, would do this is surprising. When asked if he had any reservations about reusing the story, Smith jokingly yet dismissively replied, "Obviously not."

More surprising than Smith's nonchalance towards his breach of continuity, though, is the lack of negative reaction from his fans. In surveying reactions to the film on the View Askew website, hardly a mention is made of the continuity breach. When asked specifically how they felt about the recycling of the Suzanne plot, fans replied rather nonchalantly, with responses like, "I didn't really care about the continuity break" (View Askew Message Boards).

What can account for the non-reaction of fandom to this continuity breach? It is difficult to believe that people who would fall into the classical idea of fandom espoused by Jenkins and by Harrington and Bielby would not care that the coherence of their fictional universe was compromised. Smith, fans, though, seem to be operating under a set of rules that have gone largely unexplored by fan theorists. Kevin Smith fandom (and, likely, Smith himself) is unconcerned with this continuity breach because they have seen it before in a narrative manner that Smith has primed them to expect. Smith's fandom has evolved, having less in common with comics fandom and other traditional notions of fan communities and more in common with the culture that has coalesced around *Star Wars*[26].

Star Wars culture has gone largely unexamined by academia, probably as a result of the politics it is largely held to espouse.[27] In the book *Future Tense*, author John Brosnan notes that "the most serious criticism of *Star Wars* is that it embodies Nazi mythology" (Brosnan, 263). In his book *The Science Fiction Audience*, Henry Jenkins dismisses fans of *Star Wars* as non-engaging in relation to the text, and appears to largely attribute that to the film's fascistic overtones. Jenkins prefers the fandom of *Star Trek*, the utopian themes of which, he claims, lead to a more egalitarian fan community. And, though it is unspoken by Jenkins, there is an implication that George Lucas' looming presence over the *Star Wars* property and the exploitative merchandising that has accompanied it is perfectly in line with these fascistic themes.

Jenkins and other authors writing on fandom neglect a fundamental aspect of *Star Wars* fan culture, however. As the release hype and anticipation surrounding *Star Wars: Episode I* (20th Century Fox, 1999) showed, *Star Wars* fandom is massive, and includes people who would not normally belong to a cultish, *Star Trek*-like fan community. This is due to an inherent difference between the *Star Wars* and *Star Trek* narrative universes. Understanding the difference between these is necessary to understanding the fan's acceptance of Smith's continuity breach. The difference is in each narrative's approach to the concept of 'canon.' Canon, as most often used in to science fiction franchises, refers to the texts that can be considered 'true' to the narrative at large. Texts that fall outside of the canon are often ancillary materials, such as novels, games and comics that use the franchise's name and characters, but without contributing stories that the main narrative need recognize as 'true.'

In the *Star Trek* universe, along with the *Dr. Who* and, to a lesser degree, comic book universes, fans have always innately accepted the fact that the primary texts (in the case of *Trek*, television shows and films) were the trumping authority in matters of continuity. But there has always been a certain understanding that none of the novels, comics, games, etc. will ever be rendered untrue by the primary texts. Instead, they will only be irrelevant to future, more strictly canonical stories.

Due to the limited number of primary *Star Wars* texts, combined with the relatively small amount of the 'universe' displayed in the films (the original trilogy spans about four years of narrative time, but references are made to events that take place long before that), there was a significant desire on the part of fans to fill in the gaps, both pre-*Star Wars* and post-*Return of the Jedi*. George Lucas understood this and quickly commissioned both prequels (novels detailing the adventures of a young Han Solo) and sequels (a Marvel comic taking place after the events of the films). Forays into other media followed, including an animated series, a *Star Wars* network special, and a series of video games. It was understood, however, that Lucas had plans for both the backstory and the future of the *Star Wars* universe. Thus, it was understood by fans, and, eventually, explicitly stated by Lucas, that he was the final authority in matters of canon, and the stories he would tell would automatically negate any conflicting stories. As this was common knowledge among fans, this led to their adopting different approaches to different texts. The less canonical the text, the more arcane knowledge of that text's narrative situations and characters became. As such, fans could determine their own level of involvement in the stratum of texts. If a fan wished only to involve him or herself with the films, said fan was in no danger of missing out on any details in the lower strata that would affect their understanding or enjoyment of the films. The basic strata of the *Star Wars* canon is represented as follows.

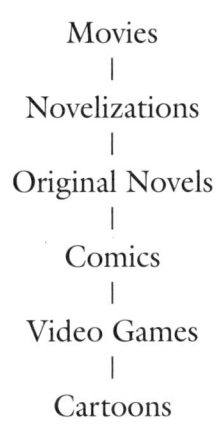

Movies
|
Novelizations
|
Original Novels
|
Comics
|
Video Games
|
Cartoons

Note that this hierarchy is approximately analogous to the size of each text's audience (with the exception of video games). In the *Star Wars* model, as a rule, a lower level text cannot contradict a higher-level one, whereas texts can always contradict the narrative of lower texts.[28]

The ability to determine one's own level of investment in the *Star Wars* universe is the fundamental difference between *Star Wars* fandom and most other types of media fandom. Series like *Star Trek* and *Dr. Who* require knowledge of not only TV shows, which constitute many hours of continuity, but also of feature films and, occasionally, novels and/or comics. The overarching narrative is much more involving, and those who would be fans must then become more deeply involved. An example of this is the knowledge of *Star Trek* history that is needed to understand the plot of *Star Trek II: Wrath of Khan*, or the story behind *Star Trek: First Contact*, which draws upon plot points from both the original series, the *Next Generation* series and the previous films. The obviousness of the depth of the narrative in *Star Trek* invites only fans that are willing to fully engage that narrative. The relative ease with which one can fully engage the primary texts of the *Star Wars* canon, however, accounts for the much larger *Star Wars* fandom.

Remember that this arose due to Lucas' lack of direct involvement with the *Star Wars* universe. When other authors were creating narratives within a highly-developed continuity that had a rabid fanbase, and when it was necessary for Lucas to retain the ultimate authority to make his own decisions about the narrative of future films, a hierarchy had to be established. Essentially, this represents a way around continuity errors and contradictions.

Given the respect that Smith has shown for the *Star Wars* universe in the past, and especially considering the near-constant references to Lucas' narrative in *Jay and Silent Bob Strike Back*, it is unsurprising that Smith would turn to that model. The first signs of this break with traditional comic continuity in favor of the stratified canon of *Star Wars* came in the *Clerks* cartoon, which was, given the outrageous situations and self-referentiality, obviously non-canon to the View Askewniverse. The break did not go unnoticed by fans, who debated the canonical status of the cartoon online. It became clear, though, that the films and comics existed on one level of canon, while the cartoon existed on a lower level. *Jay and Silent Bob Strike Back* introduces another level of canon, as the doubling of the Suzanne story would seemingly place the comics between the films and the cartoons.

It should be noted, of course, that, while Lucas asserted a primary authorship over other authors who were creating narrative within his 'universe,' Kevin Smith is the sole creator of all of the Askewniverse narratives to date. Any contradictions, then, cannot be explained away by asserting the validity of one author's story over another, as can happen in *Star Wars*-based narratives. It would seem that his fandom would reject this contradictory move. Indeed, this does happen in fandom, as many obsessive fans populate media websites like Ain't-It-Cool-News, trying to divine instances in the *Star Wars* prequels in which Lucas is contradicting the original trilogy.[29] Why then, do Smith's fans not react in a similar manner? Smith's fans accept this stratification, it could be argued, due to the fact that Smith has achieved a level of success within fandom that would place him beyond reproach. Smith has been officially embraced by *Star Wars* fandom, having graced the cover of the official publication of Lucasfilm, *Star Wars Insider*. The recent special issue of *Wizard* devoted entirely to Smith's work proclaimed, "*Wizard* is proud to spotlight independent film superstar/comic creator/American hero Kevin Smith as he prepares his newest movie, *Jay and Silent Bob Strike Back*" (*Wizard Kevin Smith Spectacular*, 1). Smith has been the guest of honor at every major comic convention in America. He was asked to host a Sci-Fi Channel special on *Star Wars*. Indeed, in many ways, he seems to have usurped George Lucas' deity-like status in the fan community. Smith's accessibility to fandom, in contrast to Lucas' seeming reluctance to engage fans would seem to play a role in this, as well. The official anointing seems to have come in the February 2002 *Wizard*, which featured a contest in which readers could have their short films judged by "God among fanboys, Kevin Smith."

Smith's future within fandom seems well-established, as he plans to keep writing comics for the foreseeable future. And since he has claimed to have retired the Askewniverse, it is not hard to imagine that his fandom will spend years waiting for him to emerge with a new Jay and Silent Bob film, much as *Star Wars* fans did between the time of *Return of the Jedi* and *The Phantom Menace*. The community that has coalesced around him is not likely to disappear in the near future.

This, it seems, is key to understanding why Smith moves away from the strict confines of comic fandom to the more accessible *Star Wars* model, and, also, why he is retiring his Askewniverse. In *Jay and Silent Bob Strike Back*, Smith has returned to the studio's dictum handed him while in production on *Mallrats*—'play it wide.' While Smith's latest film ultimately failed to appeal to a mass audience while in the theaters, barely topping *Dogma*'s $30 million gross, the rejection of continuity and the broader scope of the film's comedy seem to show that Smith, confident in the continuance of his fanbase, is moving in a more mainstream direction. Smith has become a regular guest on the touchstone of mainstream popular culture, *The Tonight Show*. He is producing a series of short comedic documentaries for the talk show, entitled "Roadside Attractions." Appearing both in the shorts and on the show to introduce them, Smith seems to be making a concerted effort to introduce himself to a mainstream audience that is unfamiliar with his films. The director has even premiered a short film on the show starring Dante and Randall, entitled "The Flying Car," which essentially plays as a profanity-free *Clerks* scene, featuring the pair debating pop culture minutiae. Commenting on the debut of the short, Smith proudly stated that more people had seen it than had ever seen his films in theaters. Smith, it would appear, has desires to be recognized outside of the realms of fandom and film buffs, and is taking steps toward that end.

In addition, however, it seems that Smith is also interested in bringing fan culture to the masses. He and artist Joe Quesada collaborated on a comic book rendition of the meeting and courtship of Smith and Jen Schwalbach that was published in the Sunday *New York Times*. Smith was involved in Marvel Comics' highly promoted 9-11 benefit books, *Heroes* and *Moment of Silence*. In June of 2002, Smith became the first guest to appear on *The Tonight Show* to promote a comic book—his new Spider-Man mini-series *The Evil that Men Do*. He has been interviewed by mainstream publications ranging from *USA Today* to *Maxim* about his love of comics and his involvement in the industry. Smith even made an outreach to cineastes on behalf of fandom with an editorial in the July/August issue of *Film Comment* in which he praised *Star Wars Episode II: Attack of the Clones*.

As for Smith's future with the critics, the relative success of *Jay and Silent Bob Strike Back* seems to suggest that he has finally gotten past the stigma of *Mallrats* with mainstream critics. In addition, it would appear that the laying aside of the Askewniverse and the return to a more personal mode of storytelling promised at the end of *Chasing Amy* has finally come to pass. Whether or not critics respond in kind is, of course, impossible to predict.

Conclusion

This book has examined the construction of the author 'Kevin Smith' through the dialogic interaction of film critics, Smith's fans and Smith himself. In doing so, it has detailed the creation of separate author biographies in the eyes of fans and of critics, tracing those biographies' respective influence on and response to Smith and his films. It has also examined the instances in which these biographies have been brought into contact within Smith's films and publicity, whether in seeming competition (*Chasing Amy*) or in co-existence, as more recent events suggest.

This study speaks primarily to three broader issues in film studies: the nature of authorship, the current practices of the film industry and the reception of films by different audiences. To first address questions of authorship, this paper has closely examined the relationships of three institutions which interact to create the author 'Kevin Smith'—film critics, fandom and the filmmaker. Through a continual renegotiation of Smith's biographical legend, each of the three affects the extratextual (and, in Smith's case, the textual) output of each of the others. As noted in the introduction, the idea that authorship can be constructed through the interaction of several factors is not new, having been explored by Robert Kapsis in relation to Hitchcock and by Barbara Klinger in her examination of Douglas Sirk's reception. This paper argues, though, in that the case of Kevin Smith, this interaction is much more of an ongoing negotiation. While Klinger, for the most part, examines the textual interpretations created after Sirk ceased making films, the interaction described here is much more dynamic, with the filmmaker, Smith, in constant dialogue with those who are in dialogue with his texts. Thus, in Smith's case, in addition to tracing the changing interpretations of a director's oeuvre over time, one must also examine the texts in light of their having been produced in full awareness of those interpretations. Reception, then, becomes a causal factor in the production of Smith's films. This self-awareness of authorship is something that could certainly be examined in any established filmmaker working within the modern American industry, as the unrelenting publicity machine and crucial significance of opening weekend grosses demands that the director be accessible to those who will both criticize and consume the text.

The approach to authorship raised above also raises questions in regard to the near-immediate 'branding' of new directors by critics and/or fans with generic and/or thematic labels and expectations. This book has detailed the manner by which Smith has both accepted and counteracted this branding. Indeed, the opening pages recounted Andrew Sarris' praise for Smith's ability to 'market himself,' i.e. to formulate and capitalize on his brand. The critical establishment clearly has a crucial role to play defining how niche filmmakers are understood by their audiences. But we can also ask, in what ways do other directors react to this process? And how does this branding affect the critical and audience receptions of their films?

Smith's savvy marketing of his biographical legend also raises issues concerning aspects of the modern Hollywood film promotion. Smith's unique online presence aims to further his career in a way that has been groundbreaking in the film industry. Even today, the number of established directors with a personal web presence numbers in only the dozens. David Lynch (*www.davidlynch.com*), Peter Greenaway (*www.petergreenaway.org*), Alex Cox (*www.alexcox.com*), Luc Besson (*www.luc-besson.com*) and Alex Proyas (*www.proyas.com*) are perhaps the best known of the other directors with websites, and it must be acknowledged that each of these is, in his own way, a niche director. Why are niche directors drawn to the web in a way that more mainstream directors are not? In taking their marketing into their own hands, it seems that these directors could, like Smith, be actively courting a community of fans.

Smith's attempts to appeal to a niche market raises another industrial question, as well. While this paper has explored in detail the impact of the comics industry on the career of Kevin Smith, his impact on the comics industry, being largely beyond the scope of this thesis' focus on biographical legend, could be explored in depth. Smith has been credited by some as having sparked an upswing in comics readership after a steady 6-year decline. Online columnist Park Cooper, decidedly not a fan of Smith's, wrote "I report to you that the industry has been saved...To my eternal shame, by sophomoric, juvenile, poop-jokes-and-penis-jokes-are-funny, Kevin Smith...But saved nonetheless" (*Silver Bullet Comics* website). Smith's success in the comics field has also led to an outreach on the part of the comics industry to Hollywood talent. Currently, J. Michael Strascynski, creator of the television series *Babylon 5*, screenwriter Bob Gale and television writer Ron Zimmerman are all employed by Marvel Comics, all following the trail that Smith blazed. Industrial studies of the comics industry are woefully lacking. An examination of Kevin Smith's impact on the industry could prove revealing and would be an excellent starting point for an analysis of the modern comics business, and the ways in which authorship, biographical legend and fandom impact that industry as well.

In terms of reception, Smith's relationship to fandom, though unique among filmmakers, prompts questions about the nature of fandom itself. In contrast to the traditionally fan-centric, egalitarian theories of fandom (espoused by Jenkins, Harrington, et al), the Smith model suggests a much more calculated manipulation of fan communities. On one hand, Smith's status as a producer of fan texts can be seen as the pinnacle of the fan-produced texts. His blatant manipulations of the fan communities that arise around his work could be an extension of his insider knowledge of what it is like to be a fanboy. Indeed, many fans would seem to approach Smith in this way. On the other hand, Smith's unrepentant milking of his fanbase in the form of merchandising and cross-promotion would seem to suggest a much more exploitative, capitalistic motivation behind his fanbase-building machinations.

The ideas of this conflict within Smith's biographical legend is at the heart of this paper's examination of the 'dueling personas' Smith developed, and nowhere was this more apparent than in the construction of *Chasing Amy*. That film also brings into play the conflict between the creative endeavor and the capitalistic impulse. Certainly, Smith can be seen to negotiate that dichotomy throughout his films. Though *Chasing Amy* presents creativity as triumphing over 'selling out', Smith himself certainly has not been above profiting from merchandising and marketing his creations. More than any other filmmaker with his 'independent' cache, he seems comfortable with the coexistence of these two drives. Smith, then, can be seen as an aberration among contemporary filmmakers or as someone who is more upfront about catering to the capitalistic side of the business than filmmakers who are more often thought of as 'artists' than businesspeople.[30] This question is in no way unique to Smith's situation. Rather, the conflict between art and finance is central to any discussion of film as commercial entertainment. Smith's apparent comfort with this dichotomy, and his skill at pleasing those on both the largely commercial enterprise of fandom and the artistically invested critical establishment, is perhaps the facet of his biography that ultimately proves most fascinating.

Notes

1. The term extratextual will herein be used to describe the discourses regarding Smith and his films that take place outside of the films themselves. This is similar to what theorist Gerard Genette has dubbed *paratext*, but, for the purposes of my argument, I feel that the boundary between Smith's films and the subsequent (and preceding) discourse is an important one to maintain.
2. The IFP is the largest association of independent film-makers in the United States, with over 3,500 members. Aside from the IFFM, the IFP also offers workshops and panel discussions (Levy, 47).
3. Some critics, in fact, saw the security camera connection as a deliberate aesthetic choice on the part of Smith.
4. As an aside, I see *Clerks* as an early expression of the malaise that David Fincher would go on to parody or give voice to (depending on your point of view) in *Fight Club* (20th Century Fox, 1999).
5. Smith may have thought that critics would embrace his nostalgic, loving look at the forgotten genre of the sex comedy, as genre revivals tend to garner respect for their efforts, if nothing else.
6. I will be using the term 'fanboy' to describe the persona that Smith creates for himself in *Mallrats*, as this is a term that Smith has, at times, used in reference to himself. While the term 'fanboy' is inherently a gendered one, 'fanboy' as applied to Smith's persona and to the fan base it helps to construct should not be understood as solely a

male moniker. While a large number of Smith's fans are indeed male, a significant, even surprising proportion is female. Smith was recently named one of "The Men We Love" by *BUST*, an alternative women's magazine. The author writes, "Kevin Smith creates female characters whom I can identify with...[he] gives girls like me a voice in the movies, and I love him for that" (McAndrew, 81).
7. The *Clerks* shooting script contains two mentions of comic books. Both are set directions that note that a comic book should appear in the scene, though neither appear in the finished film.
8. Though Brodie is the protagonist of the finished film, that was not always the case. In the original script, Brodie was much more of a secondary character to T.S.' protagonist role. Brodie occupied a place in the film roughly analogous to Randall in *Clerks*—the protagonist's id, the comic relief. Based on the strength of Lee's performance as Brodie, however, Smith bolstered the role.
9. The only aspect of Smith's *Clerks*-era biography that could rival it would be the $27,000 budget. A return to lower budgets was also a point of praise for *Chasing Amy*.
10. It is interesting to note that, at the time of filming, Allred, Quesada and Palmiotti were all independent artists, contrasting them with the Stan Lee cameo in *Mallrats*, as Lee is the father of corporate, work-for-hire comics. This contrast seems to be in line with *Chasing Amy*'s thematic concerns.
11. The death of Julie Dwyer serves, seemingly by design, as the marker of chronology in Smith's first three movies. Only those who know the name of a character never shown in the films are clued into the temporal relationship of the films to each other.
12. The text of all of the mock articles was written by Smith himself (View Askew website).
13. Though Banky's name is also a lift from *The Catcher in the Rye* (Coach Ed Banky), the alliterative closeness of the

name to Lee's earlier fanboy incarnation is, to my mind, more significant.
14. The cover seems based on *Batman: A Death in the Family*, a story in which Batman's partner Robin was killed. Ironically, the decision to kill Robin was made based on the votes of fans.
15. By comparison, at least.
16. Awarded to the film *Shadow Hours* (2000) by Isaac Eaton.
17. I've always assumed that this is Smith's way of rectifying the anachronistic fact that all of the Quick Stop patrons in *Clerks* simply request 'a pack of cigarettes,' and Dante seems to know exactly what they want.
18. Smith's draft would eventually be discarded once director Tim Burton and star Nicolas Cage became attached to the project, as Burton chose to start from scratch.
19. Of course, as any superhero comic book fan will tell you, death is rarely a permanent state-of-being in comics.
20. This information comes from the study of boards archived since August of 1999. Unfortunately, all previous boards were lost in a system crash and are not archived anywhere.
21. A few critics mention Smith's involvement in the comic book industry and/or his ownership of a comic shop (Andrew Sarris and Amy Taubin, for example). None in the mainstream media, however, have commented on the content of said comics, calling into question whether they have actually read them.
22. It is also interesting to note that *NewsAskew* saw Smith's 'roots' as being the 'balls to the wall comedy' of *Mallrats* instead of 'personal stories,' as the latter aspect of Smith's filmmaking clearly predates the former.
23. Note that even Holden the *artiste* drops a *Star Wars* reference here.
24. Recall Smith's aforementioned apologetic quote regarding his lack of personal inspiration for *Mallrats*: "If I were going to make a personal movie…it would have been about traveling from festival to festival with a first film."

25. That it took Roger Ebert five films to realize that the same characters and locations kept resurfacing in Smith's films can perhaps be forgiven, given the sheer volume of films he must watch.
26. Material regarding the nature and idiosyncrasies of *Star Wars* fandom is drawn from the author's own experiences within the subculture, unless otherwise noted.
27. A notable exception is Will Brooker's excellent *Using the Force: Creativity, Community and Star Wars Fans*.
28. This discussion of *Star Wars* canon applies to the status of the canon before the re-releases of the original trilogy in 1997 and the recent prequels. For an intriguing analysis of the now-shifting hierarchies of texts in the *SW* universe see Chapter 5 of Brooker's *Using the Force*.
29. The one break that seems to irritate *Star Wars* fans the most is the lack of recognition on the parts of Obi Wan Kenobi and the droids C-3PO and R2-D2 in the original film, despite the fact that they meet in *Episode I*.
30. In this way, the scene in *Jay and Silent Bob Strike Back* in which Gus van Sant eschews his directorial duties on *Good Will Hunting 2: Hunting Season* in favor of counting a large pile of cash can be seen not only as a good-natured jab at van Sant's recent career path, but on Smith's own negotiation of art vs. commerce.

Bibliography

Allen, Robert C. and Douglas Gomery. *Film History: Theory and Practice*. New York: Alfred A. Knopf, 1985.

Ansen, David. "Boy Meets Lesbian." *Newsweek*. April 7, 1997, 75.

Beifuss, John. "Geek's Revenge." *The Commercial Appeal (Memphis, TN)*. 25 August 2001, E1.

Bordwell, David. *The Films of Carl-Theodor Dreyer*. Berkeley: University of California Press, 1981.

Brick, Scott. "The Wizard Q&A: Kevin Smith." *Wizard*. April 1998, 82-6.

Brodie, John. "Boston Uncommon." *Premiere*. January 1998, 81-84.

Brodie, John. "Miramax Crazy About 'Amy'." *Daily Variety*. 26 August 1996, 1.

Brooker, Will. "Internet Fandom and the Continuing Narratives of *Star Wars*, *Blade Runner* and *Alien*." In *Alien Zone II*. London: Verso, 1999.

Brosnan, John. *Future Tense*. New York: St. Martin's Press, 1978.

Carr, Jay. "Earnest *Dogma* a Film to Believe In." *Boston Globe* 12 November 1999, D1.

Carver, Benedict and Oliver Jones. "Weinsteins Find Unorthodox Way 'Round 'Dogma' Dilemma." *Daily Variety*. 8 April 1999, 1.

Chernoff, Scott. "Chasing Chewie: A Conversation with Kevin Smith." *Star Wars Insider*. November/December 2001, 4-16.

Clark, Mike. "Rolling Laughs Redeem Jay and Bob's Latest Road Trip." *USA Today.* 23 August 2001, E1.

Cook, Pam. "The Point of Self-Expression in Avant-Garde Film." In *Theories of Authorship.* Ed. John Caughie. London: Routledge, 1981, 271-281.

Corrigan, Timothy. "Authorship and the New Hollywood." In *The New American Cinema*, Jon Lewis, ed. Durham, NC: Duke University Press, 1998.

Dini, Paul. "View Anew." *Wizard Special: Kevin Smith Spectacular.* August 2001, 4-5.

Duritz, Jr., Clinton. "A Conversation with Writer and Director Kevin Smith." *Film History* 8: 237-248.

Ebert, Roger. "Big-Budget Boredom; *Mallrats* Makes Us Miss *Clerks*'." *Chicago Sun-Times.* 20 October 1995, 45.

Ebert, Roger. "*Clerks* Gets Behind the Counter in Workaday World." *Chicago Sun-Times.* 4 November 1994, 23.

Ebert, Roger. "*Jay and Silent Bob Strike Back.*" *Chicago Sun Times.* 24 August 2001, 31.

Ebert, Roger. "Once in Love with *Amy*, the Eternal Triangle Gets a New Edge." *Chicago Sun-Times.* 18 April 1997, 35.

Ebert, Roger. "Sing, Oh Sinners!; *Dogma* Provides Food for Thought in Catholics." *Chicago Sun-Times.* 12 November 1999, 33.

Gaines, Allison. "'Chasing' Down the Rumors." *Entertainment Weekly.* November 28, 1997, 87.

Gleiberman, Owen. "Loose Canon." *Entertainment Weekly.* 12 November 1999, 47.

Gunning, Tom. *The Films of Fritz Lang.* London: British Film Institute, 2000.

Harrington, C. Lee and Denise D. Bielby. *Soap Fans.* Philadelphia: Temple University Press, 1995.

Harris, Dana. "Lions Gate to Clown Around, Get 'Vulgar'." *Daily Variety.* 18 September 2000, 22.

Harrison, Eric. "Slacker Satire." *The Houston Chronicle.* 24

August 2001, D1.
Hoberman, J. "No Exit." *Village Voice*. 25 October1994, 57.
Hornblower, Margot. "King of Xer Cinema." *Time*. 9 June 1997, 68.
Horton, Robert. "Snoochie Boochies: The Gospel According to Kevin Smith." *Film Comment*.
November/December 1999, 60-5.
Hutchins, Chris. "Dreaming of a 'Clerks' Christmas." *Wizard*. December 1998, 27.
"It Dirt Disher: Kevin Smith." *Entertainment Weekly*. 29 June 2001, 105.
Jenkins, Henry. "'Do You Enjoy Making the Rest of Us Feel Stupid?':
Alt.tv.twinpeaks, the Trickster Author, and Viewer Mastery."
In *Full of Secrets: Critical Approaches to Twin Peaks*, David Lavery, ed. Detroit: Wayne State University Press, 1995.
Jenkins, Henry. *Textual Poachers: Television Fans and Participatory Culture*. New York: Routledge, 1992.
Jensen, Jeff. "Mr. Smith Goes to Hollywood." *Entertainment Weekly*. 24 August 2001, 104.
Jensen, Jeff. "Saving Grace." *Entertainment Weekly*. 26 November 1999, 37.
Jones, Oliver. "Lions Gate Acquires 'Dogma'." *Variety*. 20-26 September 1999, 18.
Kapsis, Robert E. *Hitchcock: The Making of a Reputation*. Chicago: University of Chicago Press, 1992.
Kenny, Glenn. "Jay and Silent Bob Strike Back." *Premiere*, September 2001, 86.
"Kevin Smith Watch." *Wizard*. October 1999, 27.
Klinger, Barbara. *Melodrama and Meaning*. Bloomington: Indiana University Press, 1994.
Kornblum, Janet. "Director not so silent on *Strike Back* site." *USA Today*. 23 August 2001, D3.
Kornblum, Janet. "The intricate plot behind elaborate 'A.I.'

Web mystery." *USA Today.* 22 June 2001, E1.

LaSalle, Mick. "Kevin Smith's Religious Experience." *San Francisco Chronicle.* 31 October 1999, 50.

Levy, Emanuel. *Cinema of Outsiders.* New York: New York University Press, 1999.

Lumenick, Lou. "Convenience Store Coppola." *The Record.* 27 March 1994, E1.

Maslin, Janet. "Cool Dudes in a Cosmological Mood." *New York Times.* 12 November 1999, E20.

McAndrew, Kat. "The Men We Love: Kevin Smith." *BUST.* Fall 2000, 81.

McLauchlin, Jim. "Action!" *Wizard.* September 2001, 30-3.

McLauchlin, Jim. "*Clerks* Register Major Sale." *Wizard.* July 1999, 70.

McLauchlin, Jim. "Hollywood Heat." *Wizard.* October 2001, 40-47.

Merritt, Greg. *Celluloid Mavericks.* New York: Thunder's Mouth Press, 2000.

Moon, Eileen. "A Store Clerk's First Film Earns a Festival Showing." *New York Times.* 30 January 1994, 13NJ-1.

Moore, Roger. "Silent Bob Speaks." *The Houston Chronicle.* 26 August 2001, 'ZEST' 10.

Morrison, Grant and Mark Millar (w), and Steve Yeowell (a). "Four." *Skrull Kill Krew* #4. December 1995, Marvel Comics.

Pearson, Lars. "Market Watch." *Wizard.* December 1998, 130.

Pierson, John. *Spike, Mike, Slackers & Dykes.* New York: Hyperion, 1995.

Preston, David Lee. "The Auteurs Behind the Counter." *Washington Post.* 7 November 1994, D1.

Pustz, Matthew. *Comic Book Culture: Fanboys and True Believers.* Jackson: University of Mississippi Press, 1999.

Rea, Steven. "Chasing Kevin." *Calgary Herald.* 22 April 1997, C7.

Rothman, Cliff. "'Dogma' opens in New York to Protesters' Jeers, Audience Cheers." *Los Angeles Times*. 6 October 1999, F2.

Sarris, Andrew. *The American Cinema*. New York: E.P. Dutton & Co., 1968.

Sarris, Andrew. "The Next Scorsese: Kevin Smith." *Esquire*. March 2000, 218.

Sawhill, Ray. "A Talk With Pauline Kael." *Newsweek Extra*. Summer 1998, 93-4.

Senreich, Matthew. "The Wizard Q&A: Marvel Knights." *Wizard*. October 1998, 50-4.

Smith, Chris. "Register Dogs." *New York*. 24 October 1994, 50-3

Smith, Kevin. "Aaaiieee, the Jury." *Premiere*. May 2000, 50-2.

Smith, Kevin. *Clerks & Chasing Amy: Two Screenplays*. New York: Hyperion, 1997.

Smith, Kevin. *Dogma: A Screenplay*. New York: Grove Press, 1999.

Smith, Kevin (w) and Mike Allred (a). "Bluntman & Chronic: 'The Derris Affair' Part 1." *Oni Double Feature* #12. May 1999, Oni Press.

Smith, Kevin (w), Phil Hester (p) and Andre Parks (i). *Clerks: The Lost Scene*. December 1999, Oni Press.

Smith, Kevin (w) and Duncan Fegredo (a). *Jay & Silent Bob* #1. July 1998, Oni Press.

Smith, Kevin (w) and Duncan Fegredo (a). *Jay & Silent Bob* #2. October 1998, Oni Press.

Smith, Kevin (w) and Duncan Fegredo (a). *Jay & Silent Bob* #3. December 1998, Oni Press.

Smith, Kevin (w) and Duncan Fegredo (a). *Jay & Silent Bob* #4. October 1998, Oni Press.

Smith, Kevin (w) and Jim Mahfood (a). *Clerks: Holiday Special*. December 1998, Oni Press.

Smith, Kevin (w) and Jim Mahfood (a). *Clerks: The Comic Book* #1. May 1998, Oni Press.

Smith, Kevin (w), Joe Quesada (p) and Jimmy Palmiotti (i).

Daredevil Visionaries: Kevin Smith. New York: Marvel Comics, 2000.
Smith, Kevin (w) and Matt Wagner (a). "Jay & Silent Bob in: Walt Flanagan's Dog." *Oni Double Feature* #1. January 1998, Oni Press.
Taubin, Amy. "Art & Industry: Rush Week." *Village Voice.* 26 October 1993, 66.
Taubin, Amy. "Before the Fall." *Village Voice.* 5 September 1995, 72.
Thomas, Kevin. "Smart 'Amy' Captures Essence of a Good Romantic Comedy." *The Los Angeles Times.* 11 April 1997, 12.
Tomasevskij, Boris. "Literature and Biography." trans. Herbert Eagle, in *Readings in Russian Poetics: Formalist and Structuralist Views.* Ed. Ladislav Matejka and Krystyna Pomorska. Cambridge, Mass.: MIT Press, 1971, 47-55.
"Top 10 Comics." *Wizard.* October 1998, 127.
"Top 10 Comics." *Wizard.* December 1998, 133.
"Top 10 Comics." *Wizard.* February 1999, 127.
"Top 10 Comics." *Wizard.* July 1999, 117.
"Top 10 Creators: Writers." *Wizard.* October 1998, 125.
"Top 10 Creators: Writers." *Wizard.* December 1998, 131.
"Top 10 Creators: Writers." *Wizard.* February 1999, 125.
"Top 10 Creators: Writers." *Wizard.* July 1999, 115.
"Top 10 Creators: Writers." *Wizard.* October 1999, 123.
Torres, Vanessa. "MTV Docu to Detail '90s Movie Moments." *Daily Variety.* 27 May 1999, 21.
Tulloch, John and Henry Jenkins. *Science Fiction Audiences.* New York: Routledge, 1995.
Turan, Kenneth. "'Clerks' Shines Like a Gem in a Five-and-Dime Store." *Los Angeles Times.* 19 October 1994, F1.
Turan, Kenneth. "Mallrats No Match for Ultra-Low-Budget Clerks." *Los Angeles Times.* 20 October 1995, F2.
Turan, Kenneth. "Sundance Surprises." *Los Angeles Times.* 31 January 1994, F1.

"Vanguard Dialogue: Chris Rock & Kevin Smith." *Premiere.* October 1999, 98.
Wilonsky, Robert, "Fanboy Theater." *Houston Press.* 23 August 2001, 50.
Wizard Special: Kevin Smith Spectacular. August 2001.
Wood, Brian and Warren Ellis, introduction. *Channel Zero.* San Francisco: AiT/Planetlar, 2000.

Websites Consulted

The View Askewniverse:
http://www.viewaskew.com

Clerks: Official Site:
http://www.viewaskew.com/clerks/index.html

Mallrats: Official Site:
http://www.viewaskew.com/mallrats/index.html

Chasing Amy: Official Site:
http://www.viewaskew.com/chasingamy/index.html

Dogma: Official Site:
http://www.dogma-movie.com

The View Askew Message Board:
http://www.viewaskew.com/newboard

News Askew:
http://www.newsaskew.com

Developing the Monkey by Kevin Smith:
http://www.psycomic.com

Ain't-It-Cool News:
http://www.aint-it-cool-news.com

Movie Poop Shoot:
http://www.moviepoopshoot.com

Strike Back Against Jay and Silent Bob Strike Back:
http://www.jayandsilentbobstrikeback.com

Silver Bullet Comics:
http://www.silverbulletcomicbooks.com